Death Confetti

Death Confetti: Pickers, Punks,
and Transit Ghosts in Portland, Oregon
© 2016 by Jennifer Robin

A Feral House book
ISBN 978-1627310307

Feral House
1240 W. Sims Way Suite 124
Port Townsend WA 98368
www.FeralHouse.com

Book design by Jacob Covey
Photo Credits: Kurt Eisenlohr, Jud Muir, Kenneth
Barton, Nick Giampietro, and Jennifer Robin

10 9 8 7 6 5 4 3 2 1

JENNIFER
ROBIN

Death Confetti

Pickers, Punks, and Transit Ghosts
in Portland, Oregon

FERAL HOUSE

Introduction

Well...*Death Confetti*, if you want to know what it means, it is about being caught between life and death, or more accurately, conception and death. It is being caught between a fist and a kiss, a job and a gun, a burning building and a fifty-story leap to the street. In this book it means my consciousness hovering in a sack of meat like a case of static electricity that will not quit, and I am telling you about the places I have lived, and the people I have brushed against with a combination of sexual desire and disbelief.

I'd better assert this right away before you get restless: Civilization is a nightmare-illusion, a three-dimensional spreadsheet perpetuated by machines that hypnotize meat. Our cars, our laundered sheets, our air conditioning and our lies to lovers are prayers and death rituals—depending on the hour, depending on how often we blink.

Death Confetti contains parables of smut, prophecies of the future-past. I call the time period we live in the future-past because we inhabit micro-environments, micro-identities, and use our micro-skills and seek relief with the pressing of micro-buttons; and we have learned to forget when we need to forget, and we have learned to curate virtual selves, but we are losing track, faltering; fiction gone bad!

Can you stand up and tell me who you really are? Can I tell you? Really?

I am not a normal person. No one is. I was born in Syracuse, New York, raised by a reclusive set of grandparents and a bedridden mother, and when I wasn't in school, I was warned that I must not leave the house, because they believed that agents of the white slave trade, roving street gangs, and the Mafia were teeming in the bushes, or at least within a one-block radius, ready to prey on fresh meat. You could call it a Catholic upbringing, but at times it felt as if I was studying life from a space lab, trying to figure out what people on Planet Earth did—with shaky evidence and a lot of curiosity.

Whenever I had a chance to go outdoors, say to a supermarket or to church with my grandmother (she was the driver in these circumstances) my shut-in mind would be OMNIVOROUS for any details of the outside world.

I learned to drink in as much as I could from the windows of my grandmother's car: auto mechanics smoking outside a muffler shop, African-American women in bubble-shaped kerchiefs outside a beauty salon, shaky elderly men shuffling in the snow appearing homeless and in search of a grave. The goal was to make an hourlong excursion to the outdoors last for days in my imagination. Tee-vee (which I was allowed to watch) was a pale imitation of what I saw from the car windows, or the times I was allowed to walk into banks and grocery stores with my grandmother. I was ANEMIC for the real.

Even now as I approach middle age like some sort of comet grazing the Earth's stratosphere, I find that my thirst to drink in the textures of strangers has not abated—not one bit.

When I was seventeen I left home to do what most kids from "sheltered" households do: Ingest as much poison, have as much sex, and risk my life as many times as humanly possible to understand what I was missing. I lived in Rochester, Baltimore, New York City, London, and France, before traveling across the United States to see what I could find on America's West Coast.

I accepted the invitation of a prodigal son whose father was a higher-up in an electronics empire. This boy was taking so many psychedelics that he got bent on the idea of driving his car across the country to find his guru, and ultimately, his god.

I packed light. I filled a plastic bag with a silver dress, combat boots, a pair of jeans, makeup, and printouts of the stories I had written in the past year.

"I'll help pay for gas. I'll ignore his tantrums. I bet this will be over within a week," I assured myself, thinking that in seven days' time I would magically be in San Francisco, sipping espresso with computer programmers and warlocks.

This "week" turned into a summer-long camping trip in the exclusively claustrophobic company of two hippies—rife with riddles, lectures, and role-playing to the point I felt my mind melting. We passed through San Francisco, but didn't remain. We came to a stop in Portland, Oregon.

It was November, and the fog had rolled in. I didn't plan on staying here, but I sank right in, a barnacle on a shipwreck in the rain.

A shipwreck? Yes. Portland was a small city just starting to have a taste of the advertising and tech-firm money to come. Much of the downtown area was what is affectionately referred to as "dirty old Portland"—residential motels, industrial buildings, a nonstop parade of heroin dealers coughing "Chiva? Chiva?" to a nonstop parade of addicts in Chinatown.

The city was cheap, and it was easy to find employment. Portland had clean water (fresh from mountain streams!) running from the tap. It had thriving punk and literary scenes. And similar to the zombie tee-vee shows that are all the rage these days, the artists I met would nervously eye the fringes of the city where their parents and people like their parents lived, ready to tear their eyeballs out: angry white men and women on the losing end of the logging and manufacturing industries. Until the nineties, skinheads prowled the city streets at night—so I've been told by men who grew up here and proudly state that they risked beatings to walk around in sequins, in drag, with blue hair, with black girlfriends.

Not many native Portlanders in the eighties could have dreamed of our current real-estate bubble, or of the tee-vee shows that film on location downtown, or the city's ironic-art-capital status on the world's stage, or the Silicon Valley raiders, or the rent hikes and Naked Bike Rides and Voodoo Donuts and the condos landing like spaceships in the wreckage of Victorian homes demolished with shady permits—who could conceive at the time of the change about to come?

Now, in 2015, you can find communities of Koreans, Mexicans, African-Americans, Russians, Pakistanis—but they are light-years out in the suburbs, with the metropolitan area remaining, according to the most recent census, seventy-four percent white.

Portland has an Ikea, an Apple Store, strip clubs and shopping malls, new "foodie districts" where artisan cocktails and pouches of chocolate-chipped-sake-braised fetal boar lips are served for a clientele who "works hard to play hard"—and the aging punks rage, sometimes with great eloquence, that the new standards of living have caused entire neighborhoods to be evicted on three weeks' notice.

I showed up in Portland—I can't quite say "moved"—almost twenty years to the day I type this. I was twenty-two. My hormones were at full blast. I was desperate to be at rest after months of rolling. My directives, as established at seventeen—to experience real emotion, real contact with other people, all of the things you only learn by sucking cock, smoking rock, climbing cliffs, sleeping in catacombs, getting pregnant, and making a lot of mistakes—were fully enforced at this time.

Within a year of my arrival I was playing in an electronic noise band. On and off-stage, we made—or perhaps "were"—performance art. We were in our early twenties, broke, incestuous, gobbling up psychedelic gowns from the Goodwill Bins for a dollar a pound. We were drunk on the power of dressing like life-sized carrots and speaking in tongues. I simulated birth with a red satin sheet and Play-Doh balls. I cradled the heads of strangers in my hands to the point they teared up in confusion.

For the first time in my life I felt like I had found a family of rebels—refugees from the sanctioned real. Don't get me wrong; I missed the largeness, the weirdness of the cities I left behind, but the artists I met in Portland were the reason I lingered.

I've spent the past twenty years working in vintage stores, in cafés and bars, as a magazine editor, a Greenpeace canvasser, a phone psychic, a radio dee jay, a booker of noise shows, a data-entry slave, a tutor for high school and college kids, a nanny, and a "picker"—which is a not-so-glamorous title for someone who sifts through trash to find collectible items which can be cleaned up and sold to a most appreciative audience, whether in local stores or online.

From an early age I have been obsessed with debris—both the human and the non-human kinds. To run my hands over bodies, blankets, damaged things, and figure out how they became this way, how to make sense of them, or even save them—this describes me well.

I've never been comfortable in the company of those who believe in progress and prosperity. I have been in the habit of hitching my wagon to black holes, not stars.

Perhaps it's my invisible internal defect, but I have not been able to shake this feeling:

You will not find the truth on the surface. In the broken, there is truth.

Death Confetti serves as a story of my life, but like most storytelling, it is sleight of hand—more frames of the picture are missing than are shown. I have written twenty times more material than could fit in a book like this, so I have tried to keep this short and funny, if not sweet.

In this book you will meet my family, lovers, and friends. You will also meet the abandoned people—the mentally ill, those prematurely released from prisons and detox cells and group homes—people I have lived with and sat with on public transit as we were chauffeured to unknown destinations. You will meet the tweakers who forage in my yard.

Most of the events in *Death Confetti* take place in Portland, but some are from the life I had before arriving here. My life before Portland haunts me, gives me context, and at moments, relief.

Q: How many masochists does it take to change a light bulb?

A: It never gets changed because they keep sticking their fingers in the socket!

This is *Death Confetti*.

Death Confetti is a dead-end job where grandmothers mop floors with gangrened feet on Five-Hour Energy shots.

Death Confetti is all of the nuclear reactors that will go blammo! if we DO happen to off ourselves with a plague or some other form of mass extinction.

Death Confetti is the Zonked Checker, the Crack Whore Morton Salt Girl, drone strikes by the simple syrup.

Death Confetti is block after block of small red sonic alarm lights; full-bred terriers in monogrammed bathrobes; five-hundred-dollar shoe collections; refrigerator magnets and bath tissues that leave you feeling moisturized yet fresh.

Death Confetti is a freshly homeless family ambling like the walking dead and Mama's roots are growing in, and the Chihuahua is terrified!

Death Confetti is the moment I turn to you and say: The reason the world breaks your heart is because you expect too much of it—especially the human element. Your parents will betray you. Your lovers will betray you. Your government and the very soil beneath your feet will betray you, because you dreamed of MORE, so much more that you couldn't see the beauty of the scum right in front of you.

Your fatal flaw was that you expected transfiguration from a Tootsie Roll. You know...no one really ever grows up.

—Jennifer Robin,
November 2015

man

is a strange

and subtle beast

his acts

are bold

and bruise the earth

with nightmares

Identity/Portland

WHEN I FIRST MOVED to Portland I was young and I was foolish. I was trying to wash off the layers of civilization and identity I had already accrued, and Portland was the place to do it. Downtown was rife with flophouses where on any given floor you could meet three people on SSI and two who have converted to obscure but life-changing religions. One sacrificial virgin—at LEAST one!—would be in attendance on every level of every cockroach-infested tenement because Aphrodite likes to keep the loonies occupied with fresh meat. Young and petal-tipped breasts and the aroma of urine-infested hackysacks are KEY to a complete and authentic 1990s flophouse experience.

In my first apartment, I lived in a hall that had the following residents: Two schizophrenics—one, an operatic Romanian woman who screamed with intense vibrato several hours of the day, and the other a private-eye-looking man who built a shrine to Adam and Eve with a metal bowl of his feces outside my door. On one side of me was a severely alcoholic middle-aged Mormon ex-Marine who said he was kicked out of the service for assaulting a female superior. On the other side was a nymphomaniac from New Jersey who liked her men hard and whiny, the kind of men she could dominate while insinuating to them that they had the upper hand. Living between these two was like being lodged between two fists, their knuckles tattooed with L-O-V-E and H-A-T-E.

At the end of the hall was a cute crust-punk from Europe with long blond dreadlocks, and it was his apartment that caught on fire and got us all kicked out of the place.

At this point I should also note that an obsessive man whose father was a used vacuum-cleaner salesman lived on the first floor, and when the fire happened, he gave me his sweatshirt to wear on a crisp early morning as the fire was being extinguished. I wasn't cold, but I took the sweatshirt and put it on anyway, and I could sense this guy's pride, as if I had accepted his class ring. He was very short, no more than five feet tall, with eyes like saucers of milk. He looked like he very rarely saw the light of day. I never gave the sweatshirt back. I just left it in one of the many free piles that the city was made of. I wonder if to this day he imagines I cherish his totem, carefully stored inside an airtight plastic box, and inhale from it deeply on the anniversary of "our" fire.

The ex-Marine used to stand in the hall all the time. He always kept his door open, just waiting to hear the footsteps of any of us who might emerge and be the next victim of his storytelling.

I gotta say, the man had charm. He was an archetypical Western type, a bad boy who never grew up. It was customary for him to black out and find himself with a stuffed tiger on his lap at two in the afternoon outside a synagogue or an Elmer's restaurant. Once he told me an elaborate story of the time he and his navy buddies spent a lost weekend in a brothel usually only patronized by high-level diplomats and celebrities in the south of France. He could spin a story like this for an hour by describing the lushness of the fabrics, and the flesh and the wrought iron of the chateau's gate and the top-shelf waves of booze. I can imagine his sheepish grin (so wide it was!) and his twinkling blue eyes through those Coke-bottle glasses as if he stands before me now.

Toward the end of my knowing him, he started to reform, go to AA meetings. He looked worried when I brought up tall tales (my favorite being one where he snuck inside an abandoned nuclear silo) which he no longer remembered telling.

My last meeting with him, he looked spooked. We ran into each other on a bus. I reminded him of his stories, and he acted like I was (quite literally) a devil in human guise, testing him on his past. We spent the remainder of the ride looking in different directions, the rush-hour bus packed like a capsule and creeping like a cenobite.

Urinal Big Boy

HUMANS SPEND SO MUCH TIME trying to escape their natural smells and processes. I know, who am I to talk, right? I am on many occasions doused in a cloud of perfume. As of a couple months ago, I have started doing laundry on a regular basis. For the first time ever, I even cleaned my toilet with bleach! But I remember the many exotic smells I have allowed to waft up my nose and past my uvula in a sharp U-turn before suffusing my lungs, my core, with continued life, itself.

"Continued life" smells like the very intimate processes of growth and decay that surround us. I could talk about the bus when it is cramped and coated in a wintertime condensation, and in that precise moment, where one cannot even see out the steamy window anymore, one has the crystalline realization that one is taking in the very intimate gases, and to a degree the cellular thumbprints, of every person in the chamber. If you raise your hand to wipe the condensation off the window, you will wash their very breath turned into liquid off that pane. Dare you place your hand deep in their lungs so that you can see? See that speed freak scratching his crotch with the scent of putrefied flesh fanning from his dirty gym shorts with every twitch? That liquid is his breath! See that woman squeezing her toddler's hand too hard to make it shut up when in fact it makes the toddler scream harder? It's her breath, too.

There are moments when I throw caution to the wind and wipe the window anyway.

I remember long nights with new lovers where I had to let out air. I mean THAT air, gas from the poop chute, or what some of you commonly call "farts." I am strangely sensitive to the sound of words. I never liked the word fart. "Fart." When I would try to "test" it out in discourse, it would, in reality, feel like a fart. My attempted usage of the word fart reminds me of a pubescent child, or a prudish old woman who tries to use the words "shit" or "cunt" for the very first time. It stutters out of my mouth. It modulates strangely. The glottal stop I use to cut off the "fart" comes too quickly. I try to make it sound coarse, when it actually sounds abandoned by me; an orphan the very second it was born.

How long is a new lover a new lover? Perhaps as long as you feel the drive to "hold it in." The first time I heard the term "Dutch oven" was when in France. I was with a lover and the room we were in was probably three hundred years old. The blankets were rough; the air was as dank as you would expect outside the coarse flannel blanket, and underneath, I was weary, I was bloated. I let 'er rip. Hey, the guys I was around did a lot worse than this.

My lover's head was above the blankets. I realized that so long as I held the top of the blanket very tightly to my chest, nothing would escape. Ten, twenty minutes later, when he did wake up and get out from under the covers, he discovered the smell (which was still perfectly preserved under the blanket) and said, "Ah! Dat eez like a Dootch oh-ven!"

For many years afterward I found inventive ways to let the gas out of a discreet side opening I would make in the blankets—I thought I was being so stealthy but I probably haven't fooled anyone.

I remember the first time I saw (and smelled) a urinal cake. I was fascinated by the term "urinal cake" before I even knew what one was. I was eighteen years old and at a vast outdoor concert in Baltimore. After jumping up and down with hundreds of drunk sweaty bodies, I had to find a bathroom. Being a public restroom in a park, it was a disaster area. A powdery fluorescent light showcased towel dispensers having been ripped from the walls and crushed plastic cups everywhere.

To get to the toilets with stalls, one had to dodge puddles and pass an area of smooth porcelain urinals. The sleekness of their design intrigued me. Their curves reminded me of dolphins. I liked these urinals. The smell of a urinal cake reminded me of dental products—all of those factory-made scents that are used to flavor toothpaste, or dish soap, or panty liners. I can't get enough of these industrial smells. I leaned closer to smell the urinal cake. No guys were in the room for that brief moment; I could indulge!

I inspected the urinal cakes in the long line of heads until I reached one at the end. Resting on top of this urinal was what, from a distance, looked like a doll. It was a small miniature model of the burger joint Big Boy—you know, that boy with checkered overalls and a huge poo-brown pompadour, and eyes that gleam with excitement as they spy platters of fresh meat. In fact this Big Boy was on a surfboard while simultaneously holding a platter of burgers. I had to have him—though I didn't know what I would have him for.

I washed Big Boy out in the sink with plenty of pink industrial soap, dried him, put him in my pocket. I still have that Urinal Big Boy to this day. He felt like a trophy of some sort.

Once in New York City, I was coming from a club in the meat-packing district. The thing is, it may have been hip to have clubs in the meat-packing district, but a lot of meat packing was still taking place. In one establishment, an entire basement's worth of meat had gone bad. The refrigeration must had failed at some point...several days before. The smell that emerged was clearly the smell of a whole FLOOR of rotten meat grown sentient. It literally walked down streets, crossed intersections. It had a life of its own. It hit me in the face like something supernatural and made me vomit on the spot. There are smells so bad that they make a person react immediately.

So back to the speed freak: Recently I was on bus and I saw a speed freak who had once been handsome. I add that "had once been handsome" coz it adds a narrative arc to the whole thing, doesn't it? You can imagine someone who had a lot of fun, had a lot of incredible sensations before meeting this fate, rather than a man who was always on the outside looking in. He was balding, emaciated, probably around thirty-five. He wore a Gorillaz baseball cap, a nondescript rave sweatshirt, dirty sneakers. The skin on his legs reminded me of the bark of a baobab tree, covered in a fine hair which he kept scratching. I could see sores. His eyes were a wide dustbowl blue. His mouth had a million machinations.

But what I have been saving up for last is his GYM SHORTS. The color of a discarded kleenex, a mucous gray. He could not get his hands out of his gym shorts. He had several pockets in there, and they were packed with homeless man supplies, so packed that their girth irritated his raw nerves and he had to keep shifting around the pockets for an entire forty minutes (it was a long bus ride). And every time he reached his hands into his pants (which was every ten seconds) shifting around supplies, sometimes taking them out, and scratching, scratching, scratching, he fanned the scent of crotch that had not been washed for a long time to the entire rear section of the bus. This was a powerful, private fume. Anyone who had perfume, mufflers, breath mints, face masks, or dementia—this was their time to use these devices and privately endure in the way we have been conditioned to endure.

There are so many flavors of dirt. I have traveled to countries where everything smells like dirt, an old dirt that seems ironed into every surface. This dirt is nearly creamy in its scent. It is a delicacy of dirt, mashed, vital, warm. This un-American dirt; it is like a paté produced by civilization having been overfed.

Americans, unless you have traveled, you have no idea how dense the rest of the world smells. Instead of writing more let me just ask you to imagine a city made of ambergris-dentures-whale-piss-tiger-piss-dead-rat-hairspray-junkie-tongue-mozzarella-asafoetida-chorizo-onion-eyewash-lysol-cigarillo-tomatillo-sand-baking-bread-hiatus-leprosy-poontang-diesel-sandalwood-money-shoe-birdseeds-formaldehyde-armpit-gut-pit-monkey-tongue-figs-salsa-chicken-bone-dumpster-fish-fish-fish-fruit-piss-time-piss-mud-piss-cleaning-product-piss-bag-canker-sore-fireworks-smoke-piss-ether.

Ouija/Bored

THE MINUTE YOU WALK IN, you sense something institutional about the place. The pitted concrete floor, the high ceilings, the strips of unadorned fluorescent lighting, the smell...like a hamster cage filled with spilled shaving cream...these are the qualities that make you feel as if you have descended into a zone outside of space as you know it.

The way people move in this place...you can't entirely place it... yet they shuffle, as if they are seen through the fog of a dream. The bodies are restless, yet the souls are resigned. The more you attempt to put a name to it, you are reminded of inmates getting 'outdoor time' in a penitentiary yard.

Old hands fold doilies in neatly stacked piles. Children pick up doll parts from underneath a shopping cart. A man who doesn't quite look like Elton John flips through a stack of albums on a divan, before a balding employee warns him he must get up and move. "This is not a sorting area," you hear the employee say.

Slowly, you sense a change in the air. As aimless as the eighty or so people in this room appear to be, you sense an alertness overtaking several shoppers.

They are rising from the yellow dinette set. They detach from an aisle of smoky sheets. Even the punks playing with a broken abacus are shuffling with greater urgency toward the back left corner of the room, where Mexican men with gated eyes roll away gray bins full of photo albums and dead uncle.

Over a loudspeaker, a voice barks: "Rotation, aisle nine."

In the space where the bins were, yellow tracks are visible on the floor. Something uncanny and biological is taking place.

Russian women line up in their space-age babushkas. A black woman with pomaded hair and a Race For The Cure windbreaker closes her eyes and appears to call on an inner strength. Her fists are balled like the roots of a tree, so tight you can count her tendons.

Five middle-aged white men in sports jerseys banter about the weather and their latest acquisitions. It's funny how even in a setting like this, you can sense the histories these men once had as quarterbacks and track stars.

Other, more fantastical beings twitch: A man who is independently wealthy drives up in a Mercedes fresh from getting a hair transplant. As he sifts through a pile of alligator purses he has found, the soft blond plugs at the top of his forehead begin to leak a pinkish plasma.

There is a woman who with great investment and little sleep has rendered herself a grinning skull. Skull has stuffed her shopping cart with enough sporting equipment to fill an Egyptian tomb.

Close to Skull is a twenty-something girl in a red leotard who looks like a graduate student. Her bearing is like a ballerina; her face reminds you of the young Bernadette Peters.

Patiently attending are the ice queens. They hate it here. They sell linens on Etsy and "rehabilitate" teak. In addition to their carefully coiffed hair and starched blouses, they set themselves apart from their neighbors by wearing surgical masks.

Everyone has taken a place. A hush falls over the crowd.

The Goodwill employees scream, "Ro-tay-tion!"

The pickers eye each other. Each plastic bin is nine feet long, four feet wide, filled to capacity with junk sprayed in a sickly sweet berry antiseptic.

This is the junk discarded from the Goodwill retail stores, a hodgepodge of suicide notes and soiled underwear and marginally working toaster ovens and Goodwill is STILL trying to make a buck off this garbage!

As the bins are rolled into their places between the yellow lines, several pickers are 'breaking the rules' and swiping. One of the jocks discovers that the promise of a satin baseball jacket was just a table-cloth. These early swipes are tossed back in disgust.

Once the wheels of each bin come to a halt, the tug of war *really* begins.

People get bruised. They look as if they will strangle each other. There is an aquatic quality to the motions of the arms, to the waves of debris. The pits of matter never end. New bodies dive into each pit, each bin, each black hole abandoned by the previous wave of arms, eyes, breathing holes.

Little Mexican women wriggle like kittens in sweatpants. A man with greasy black hair and shock-treatment eyes dives between the bodies, using his height to extract scraps of fabric over his neighbors' heads.

The pickers can barely hold on to all they have grabbed from the first bin, when the second bin comes rolling up. They vie for places. They swerve. Their mouths are tightened. Garbage is gold.

Five days later the Bernadette Peters of the Bins models a tattered mink stole on Ebay. The lighting...the *photoshopping*...the extravagantly applied cosmetics transform a rotting piece of leather purchased for the price of a coffee into a 365-dollar auction piece.

Sometimes I feel like America is made of millions of people in latex gloves going through gray plastic bins for every last bowling ball and earring, every pottery shard and shark tooth to sell to overseas collectors. We have lost the keys to the kingdom, and what we do is hock scraps of sacred soil to curious onlookers. Maybe one day there will be a Goodwill Bins installed in Vatican City selling soiled Pontiff's robes and the pelvic bones of long-forgotten saints.

Is garbage gold? You hear it like a mantra.

You have to be a gambler at heart. This is what I believe, though some pickers say there is an exact science to the practice, and the Bins can be worked the way a Vegas showgirl works the room for tips.

I ANSWERED THE PHONE CALL at 7 a.m.—the phone call from my Bins-buddy, Ross. He enticed me with his magic words: "Come to the Bins! You can't say no to the Bins!"

Eight hours later we sat in front of my apartment building. The coffee in our blood had expired. Our breath was turning sour. We sat in the car as if we were involved in a stakeout.

Junk threatened to suffocate us on all sides. Ross had his car so crammed with junk from the Bins that there was no longer a back seat, no longer a trunk. His car was like a parade float, a shell packed with months of accumulated matter: Garfield neckties, mohair sweaters, bits of plastic tubing, hundreds of sequined scarves, stuffed animals, and platform shoes. If anyone ever wonders what happened to Studio 54, they could speculate that it was swallowed and regurgitated inside of this car.

In my lap was a black garbage bag full of vintage wool coats, Christmas ornaments with faulty electrical wiring, and a Ouija board missing its planchette.

I had paid money for these objects, but I couldn't begin to ponder what they meant separately or in combination with each other. I was sleep-deprived. The sky was beginning to pulsate around my head. The sidewalks commenced a gentle sway.

After several hours of picking carnage, I was smug in the knowledge that my garbage bag would stretch my initial investment of twenty dollars into eighty, or even *two hundred* on a good day! My garbage bag had not yet lost its patina of mystery.

Ross joined me as I brought my haul into my ground-floor apartment. The storefront window was covered in a sheet from the Bins featuring a series of op-art cats. Our eyes were tired and we were glad that the 'curtain' was closed.

I fetched us some water and made us sandwiches and started to sift through the items in my bag. I pulled out the Ouija board and started thinking about all of the times it must have been used.

Who was its previous owner? Did it have several? I visualized a teenaged boy with a face like a moth. He wore a ruffled tux and held Black Masses in a split-level ranch house. I visualized an old man who missed his deceased cat. I visualized the sexless wife of a NASA propulsion specialist who lounged in Frederick's of Hollywood palazzo pants, and she hoped that at least ghosts would keep her company.

Whatever its uses, thoughts of the Ouija board started to fill me with a low-level anxiety.

I told Ross about my freshman year at college. I met a girl who fashioned herself as a witch. Toward the end of the semester, she stopped going to her classes and spent every day from morning to dusk talking to 'the spirits of dead children' on her board. She told me they wouldn't leave her alone.

As an avowed atheist I had no reason to fear an old piece of cardboard manufactured by the Milton-Bradley Company...yet my tension was growing. During a lull in the conversation, I picked up the board and said to Ross:

"I don't know if I should keep it."

"Get rid of it!" he said, "I would have never picked up the thing."

"The thing is, now it *knows* we picked it up."

"We? Don't get me involved."

As children of the seventies, both Ross and I grew up on horror movies where ventriloquist's dummies and kitchen appliances would come to life, as if possessed by malevolent forces from beyond. No inanimate object was safe.

"It's going to stick to us!" Ross said.

"Suppose I left it out on the street corner," I speculated, "...but no. It would be too close to me. It would detect the presence of The One Who Brought It Here."

We both imagined the board scurrying down the sidewalk and slipping through the crack under my door, ready to greet me the next morning with an air of perkiness, as if expecting a cup of coffee and a danish.

Ross said, "You have to take it further away!"

"I know!" I smiled at him. "I could give it to you and you could bring it back to the Bins tomorrow!"

"I'm not letting it back in my car!"

My mind started calculating exactly how far I would have to take the board so that it would be attracted to the volatile energies of a new 'exciting' mind.

"I know! The Safeway phone booth!"

The downtown Safeway was about to be remodeled, and was experiencing the last stages of decay before being completely torn down.

Its physical decay seemed to attract a clientele of addicts, crust-punks and schizophrenics who would stand near the pay phone at all hours. Like the pickers at the Bins, these pay-phone ghosts were lined up for their own flavors of salvation. Almost every time I'd walk by there, a homeless kid would try to sell his food stamp card to me for drug money.

I briskly walked over to the phone booth, speaking like a coach to the object in my hands. "You'll find a really good one here!" I told it.

It was as if I were putting the final touches on an art installation. Once I placed the Ouija board above the phone's oily mouthpiece, I felt that life was as it should be. Within five minutes, that board would bond with a drag queen named Darkest Nubia and my life would be at peace.

Poo Poo
Splatter Splat

IN PORTLAND THE LIGHT RAIL is called the Max. I get on the Max and a stop later a guy gets on...I guess he is at least nineteen, with his big, disused build and his reams of soft flesh and his five o'clock shadow at 2 p.m. and his legs, in blue denim going gray, that are so thick, like pipelines of tendon, like tree trunks, crossed in a madhouse ecstasy as he presses buttons on a little device. Everything these days is a "device." Even a backpack can be an explosive device, and whenever I see one abandoned on a highway median or a bus shelter, I think of the teams of plastic-wrapped security drones who will inevitably come running to inspect and remove the theoretical-explosive-backpack-device only to find empty Cheeto bags and lube and Axe cologne and Tic-Tac containers and beef jerky wrappers and dead lighters and the Library of Alexandria inside.

SO this guy, he has a tiny device in his ground-chuck hands, his hands are just curled around it, pressing and flapping, and he is like a large toddler making "Pooo! Pooo!" sounds. Nothing TOO crazy, now. He is still in the realm of stoned dudes seeking thrills. He is the baby of the family who everyone lets be a baby forever-and-ever-and-ever until he is fifty-six, and a janitor, and diabetic, and in love with the neighbors' pubescent girl with mile-wide fish eyes and lips like a soft Don Knotts.

This is he: He goes, "Poo! Poo! No!! Come back...Come back!" as the tinny speaker makes bells and casino sounds. No war game is this. It is so abstract and cute, and if something is killed it probably sighs in pleasure as you kill it. I imagine, as the man exclaims with a dizzy sort of glee, that if his mouth opened, he would expose a set of sharp and gleaming rabbit teeth. On his feet he is cushioned with enormous marshmallow-colored sneakers. They jut out at impossible, pointless angles, like a Frank Gehry building: pomp without circumstance. He is lost in the most sublime adventure; he is, as Zen masters and yoga instructors might say, following his bliss. And the lottery bells susurrate, and he cries "Poo! Poo!" again and again and "Come back! NO!" mourning, if but for a second, the loss of digital nonsense.

Dialed In

ON THE BUS: I see a homeless man appear to type into a cell phone. On closer inspection I discover that he is elaborately toying with a Dorito.

Tweaker Freds

IT IS NIGHT OUTSIDE the MEGA-grocery store. Three tweakers wheel into the parking lot, a compact black car with a "cute" skull sticker. It darts in and backs out of spaces like a drunk hummingbird, almost crashes into three other cars. When I get a look at the driver in the dimness, she is straight out of a thirties horror movie; she is the offspring of Bela Lugosi. She is a tweaker who has been tweaking a while—years, most likely. Her face isn't just hollowed out; it actually appears BROKEN, as if she has fallen and bashed in one of her cheekbones and doesn't realize it yet. How did her head get so misshapen? The way her hair is pulled back, the way she squints as if (even with wide eyes) she cannot see what is in front of her. She squints, she bobs her head. She may be seeing a thousand lampposts in the lot; a palpitating red neon sign, an evacuated life, a sack leaking blood; she is a rattle-shark; she is a buzzing pole, a saucer-mind supreme. She is driving and the men aren't. Beside her is a guy equally hollowed out, his eyes are white melting pools, his mouth is open, and perhaps cannot shut. They are picking up a guy who runs from the store, eases into the back seat, also with runny egg eyes, a gaping open mouth. How tight is the flesh over bones so that every hole grows larger? The skin can no longer encompass the skeleton that grows in power with every crystal snorted. Who wants to stay awake forever?

Date With Death

I DATE DEATH, but this is nothing new. The latest incarnation of death calls me his wife. There are parlors, stalls and halls of mirrors all over this great nation where death is introduced to death; a million little deaths pile through doors and have animated chats about the lives they run from at night.

The death I date was fresh off work and calling me on the phone. He was dropped off by a co-worker at his gate, but he wasn't ready to go in. It was a little after midnight and I could hear the booze in his voice already. He had a drink at work, maybe two, but he needed more.

He works in a bar, but after work he goes to another bar to drink away work, the faces of prosperous white families with autistic children and receding hairlines and nail-file-thin glow-screens they press instead of speaking and unwarranted anger that their halibut and French fries are not perfected in a sublime way that delivers a sense of satori, transcendence, what some call weightlessness.

Is there a plate of fries or a cocktail or a Caesar with grilled chicken that can restore the collagen on one's face or remove the cholesterol from one's heart, or the memories of compromise and suicide from one's memory bank? This on demand, ten minutes ago, for a room packed with dozens of families, microwaved foodstuffs as a means of blocking off the mouths of children, wives; like the mutes of trumpets, the mutes of food. This is what he navigates. He picks up peas from the floor and delivers straws and napkins and he is deafened by their shouts, and after hours he drinks until the blood vessels burst on his nose and his eyes look like glass panes.

I was listening to him. He was rambling. I could feel the thinness of his legs in gray denim, the lank shapes of his arms in a leather jacket, the wisps of his long brown hair as his voice began to protract like a line drawn in outer space by an enormous pencil...a loop of thread, of spittle, a voice that washes into the Milky Way, when he said: "Oh shit, someone just fired a gun in front of me. The things people do on a Saturday night. I'll call you back, baby."

A friend of mine was leaving her husband and staying at my house. I went downstairs to see her, this lady who feels like tomboy squints; a rainbow hammered into a precise shape, and I told her the man I love hung up because someone was firing a gun in front of him. It might be a drive-by, I said. It wasn't unusual for his street. He'd sit on his fire escape through the wee hours making smoke-shapes in the air, looking like a seventies detective—shirtless, sipping wine, watching people stagger, fight and run.

Portland is changing fast. It used to be that whites didn't live on his street, but in the decade my death-doll has lived there, things have changed. Condos with names that remind me of yoga poses have cropped up. A day care center called "Sensory Kids" for children with allergies to nuts and oxygen and just about everything and an artisan ice cream store and a Doctor Who-themed bar have all found their homes, have landed like spaceships from another income bracket in his neighborhood. Homeless men still make encampments in colors of brown and gray and shopping-cart silver at steep angles of the highway overpass a block from my man's place; however, the writing is on the wall.

Half an hour later he called back. He told me a bullet whizzed past his head a couple inches from the important parts. It was so close that it made his hair fly up in the air. He said the owner of the bar had a gun and was shooting at someone down the street, but to shoot the guy down the street he had to shoot past anyone in the way.

"Who knows what happened to the guy. We didn't see a body lying there. If someone got shot, maybe he's in a car and is far away now. Fuck knows where or how he is...the owner is out there like a madman shooting past the heads of his customers...that crazy fucker missed me by an inch because I moved closer to the window to hear you better on the phone."

He spoke to me from the smoking patio behind the bar, watching as men in kilts and novelty T-shirts chatted about how "off" it was that cops were there. It's kind of like the game of telephone where a shooting can happen in front of a bar and cop cars swerve up and the red and blue lights are flashing like a night-dream turned day and still the people at the back of the bar don't have much of an idea what is going on.

"Shit, you know I grew up with fucking guns all around me, I get real calm when shit like this happens. Fuck, this is reality. Violence is reality! It brings me focus. This is the real me. This is the real America...any fuckjob who can afford a gun is walking around like it's the Wild West...Well I'm ready to sit back and watch it burn! If these idiots can't hold it together anymore and wanna blow each other's heads off, let them sign their own death warrants."

"They almost signed yours, too."

"Hey I can die at any time, baby. I grew up around death. I'm not afraid of death. Why should anyone hold on so long to...what? Being a human being? I'm glad I'm getting out of here when I am! And you know everyone is blaming it on the blacks, blamin' it on the niggers, everyone's sayin' 'It's another drive-by,' but I saw it, it was the fuckin' owner pulling a gun out of his jacket and just waving it in the street. He's losing it. Fuckin' asshole wants to fire guns in a crowd of people? Well sheeit, I get calm in shitshow situations like this..."

And he told me he went inside and drank two whiskeys to top off the calm.

Karaoke night was in full swing. People kept singing and drinking, but a few regulars sensed too much weirdness in the air and were making an escape.

I would tell you the name of the bar but it isn't important. I would tell you that a lot of people called it a dive, and it was one of the last bars in the neighborhood where you could see black folks and white folks and Mexicans and hookers making a buck and mothers and young lovers and people who are punk for life, or whatever that means these days, because no one says "punk" anymore...People just wear black and have their hair shaved into mohawks and they hold down jobs but in other ways they've dropped out because this is the great migration away from America.

News Flash: A lot of America no longer believes in America, and they, great numbers, in hundreds and thousands in each city have encampments and broadcast to each other and they serve food and tend bar and cut hair and answer phones and with sleeves of tattoos that arch toward their ribs as if their pale flesh has captured souls and been dyed by them, these people call each other family in ways I have tasted, but I am a lone one who senses, even when they hold me in last call's embrace, that I am outside their reality. I no longer mourn this as much as I recognize it is truth.

These are men who practice Wicca and listen to the Clash and do stand-up comedy and some of them are bouncers, and the women have pay-for-view websites, and there are men who have lost and regained their children, and fry cooks, and a Mexican man who may be younger than me and he works long hours and always falls asleep at the bar, and the bartender who has eyes like a portrait of Jesus, so gentle, he wears a baseball cap that reminds me of anarchy, and he always has to poke this man who is nodding off, over and over again, call his name, because if no one calls his name, he is breaking the law by being unconscious in a bar.

And there is the girl who someone hurt when she was a kid. A man who was older than her did things to her and she became obsessed with the young adult novels about a girl named Anne of Green Gables, in fact she had long passages of these novels memorized and she would try to recite these and a poem by Dorothy Parker and another one from Chaucer to almost everyone who would look at her but no one wanted to look at her coz she'd show up with no money and creep up like a mouse with her round white face and her round white eyes and her hair that is sometimes black and sometimes blue like a Betty Boop without Bimbo, meekly squeezing our shoulders and speaking with a honey voice:

20

"Heyyyy...I remember you!" and asking in an even more polite way if you could just possibly buy her a two-dollar PBR because she is a little short and she has done this to all the regulars, and if you're a woman she has offered blowjobs for small cash reimbursements to your men, and she has no luck with anyone unless they just buy her the beer to make her go away because once you buy her the beer, she has two more sentences with you and then she does go away, to find the next person who might buy a beer and listen on top of it all, and she is the kind of person another person grows to love and hate at the same time, because you see what is broken in her, but you see she burned away other circuits to deal with the broken parts, like circuits of shame.

I watch as a pool game unfolds and the guy named Bobby is playing, he looks like a wise old turtle, and Marvin Gaye is on the jukebox and a nervous middle-aged white guy in denim who was once a redhead but now the fern-like growth on his head and the stubble on his chin has turned another color, and he has wire-framed glasses and who knows what he does in the daytime, but he gets too excited when he plays pool and the other guys in here are lean, and non-white, and when they play pool they glide through the air like paintings of herons, and meanwhile this white guy he is nervous, he is jumping up and down and cheering his own shots as if he is watching a football game, and he punches the air with "awwww"s and "damn"s when he misses his shots and he reminds me of the cartoon character Barney Google, with his goo-goo-goo-guh-lee eyes, they are searching for a mark, a mama, a friend, and the regulars instead are smooth, closed surfaces, and I can see it happening before it happens!

Of course, this girl, who calls herself an insect name, this nickname that is sweet and full of longing, she is going to find him, AND SHE DOES! She will not just have a beer now, she will have a bed to lie in...why not take it all the way, for another night?

An hour of drinking later and the two of them are huddled together at a wooden picnic table on the smoking patio out back, and I can feel the way she is gazing at his shoulder and he probably can't believe his luck, a girl so young, who looks so clean and eager, why is she in here, he doesn't entirely know but he cannot say no to the moment.

My man and I leave before the last drink is poured. It's a rare feat to get him out before last call because whiskey is his wish, his flesh, his home, but weird things are happening in there, and have been, and there are certain nights when the owner comes in and these guys come in who sit at a high round table on seats so tall their feet dangle off the ground, and they mean business and it looks like there will be a showdown, and sometimes a girlfriend is there, and the way these people move is like marionettes, and meanwhile the seated men are like Easter Island heads just waiting for the rest of us to leave, and an SUV-limo is outside with a lot of chrome and the lights are on and it is pumping music, and I am not a regular and sometimes the man I am with gets mad and says I know nothing about that world and I end up kissing him and rubbing my naked body on him while he's passed out on the floor of the room he rents one block away from the bar he calls his living room.

"Baby, I grew up in bars. My mother brought me in my carrier to bars. She set me down in the kitchen so she could sit with her friends and drink. The cooks would watch me...everyone watched me...I was safe."

This is the story of a lot of nights between the hours of midnight to 4 a.m. mashed up into one, because that is when the action happens, when I would make my trek to the north of the city to see the man I dated for a year but I'd have to go to his turf because he was too tired to go to mine.

"You try to work a job like mine and go across town to see your woman...I'm dead on my feet!"

"Not too dead to drink whiskey."

"This whiskey...is the only thing keeping me alive..."

I tell him I've had many jobs frying food and serving coffee and wine and the promise of my body in my twenties, and the last thing I wanted after work was to sit in bars. I wanted to make up for lost time.

"Well good ferrr you! You don't know shit about how things are now. People are different now, a hundred times worse. I go to service industry bars. Look around, this is service industry here. We're fucking *whores*. Strippers, bartenders, cooks. Everyone in this bar is a whore like me. You know how keyed up we are after we get off work? Sheeit, you wouldn't last a second at my work!"

And yet he loves me and calls me a genius, or that's what he told this guy who makes pot brownies on our very first date, when we staggered up to his room, and this brownie-baker revealed to us his taste for older ladies, and eyed me appraisingly, because after all he wasn't a day over twenty-eight and the man I knew I had to kiss said, "This woman, she's the real deal."

But that is always what we say before we know what the real deal is.

There is a woman in a metal band and her mother dated a gigolo who took her money but he had something happen to him, like he was trapped in a car naked with a rabid dog, or he was arrested for driving a car into a tree, or he was eaten alive by spiders in a trailer, I don't remember now. And there was a man who died of a coke overdose in his Chippendales underwear, and no one missed him because he was a killer of people's housecats and stored them in a trash can, and there were many fathers who only had partial custody of their children, and Pat was a lesbian who lived in Alaska but when she was young down California way she took a lot of drugs like Four Doors which makes you trip balls and fade into the furniture if you're not careful.

Between these wooden walls and neglected video game consoles people would tell each other endless stories—these, and more than these. And some didn't utter a word. Some existed in smooth and otherworldly columns of silence, as if they were in pneumatic tubes, in a queue to be sent to another floor of a vast and labyrinthine building.

And in this bar on a karaoke night that wasn't as happening as the others, the man held my waist and asked me if I was his wife and I said yes, I was ready to melt into his arms like a cheese-filled tamale, and he tilted my head back, or maybe I tilted it myself and we kissed and I thought, could it be that he is finally growing to love me more than alcohol, and of course I know he loves me, but it is a match I will never win, but maybe it is all right, less pressure on me if he just loves me on the side...

And he said, "Baby, I have something to tell you, it's serious. Come with me out back," and I thought it was going to be something having to do with love, and marriage, and who knows, I just didn't know, and I kept on drinking even though I didn't want to drink, and then he slowly silently told me at a picnic table in shadows about this couple who wanted to smoke pot with him at his place a week before and he said sure, and it was last call and they needed somewhere off the street to smoke and they all were in the kitchen and the stuff they had was so strong and he lost track of everything and must have blacked out and he woke up with a naked woman in his bed, and he said "You're not Jennifer" and she said, "No, I'm not, you said that before," and he was so sorry and he has never done anything like this before and he doesn't know how to go on, and something changed in me like I knew this would happen half of the time but then I didn't know the other half, and he said:

"You hate me now, don't you? It's over now, isn't it?"

And I said, "I don't hate you. I knew this would happen eventually."

"See? You know I'm no good. So it's over."

And I said the thing I say to men who pass out more than fuck which is, "It's not like she would've got much out of it anyway," and then I think of how for so many nights I would just wait for him to get drunk, just the right amount of drunk, but not too much so that he wouldn't be so feverish to drink and might think for two seconds about holding me.

And oh! The touching! How much of it was in my imagination? How much of it was a match made in heaven, or purgatory, or the hell of lost personalities. The lost conjoin with the lost like unattended flames.

She was a stripper I'd met in a bar downtown and I liked her back then, a year or two before, when she had green hair and a can-do personality and Liz Taylor makeup like my own. Perhaps my death-doll of a man was surprised that I knew who she was, because he felt that the world of strippers and bars was HIS, not mine—but I knew, I knew.

And he was crying at last call as we left the bar, and I held his arms and said, "I never thought of this as something that was going to be exclusive," even while he called me his wife and I said YES YES YES FOREVER and I was lying through my teeth about "I never thought of this as blah-blah-blah exclusive" but knowing the truth at the same time, this is a man who needs the love of every warm-blooded body in a crowded bar, women flock to him and rub against him and how can I blame them?

He is the orphan-confidante of the old and the young and the PEOPLE: men, women, junkies, rock stars, the homeless, the hopeless, children on the curbs, and I mean seriously he will call a cab for a molested woman or lend his couch to a buddy who cannot walk, and how? How could I ever think that he could cut off his life like Samson cut off his locks for a bride? He cannot be owned by one woman! His soul thirsts to drown in the soul-fluids of others. He is a symbiote to the wood-grain dim, the sardine quality of bodies packed in a room intimately off-gassing the pain of their days.

He calls them his babies: He folds each one in his soot-black sleeves, he kisses their kewpie-doll cheeks, their old man necks, the ones crushed daily by the specious demands of tourists and their aspirants who will never have enough; his babies are workers ground under an endless succession of moneyed pretenders who in their very constitutions cannot recognize that the temporary possession of products, the discovery of artisan bread crusts, and owning every color and tasting every flavor will not deliver peace.

Man, who are you without the night?

I polished his body as a groupie would polish a trophy, and when he was sober I was his poet, and when he was drunk I was his wife, and it was getting to the point where I could barely drink one more drop, because it no longer felt like fun, this sacrament of forgetting.

The bar was running out of booze, and fast. The owner stopped sinking money in the place. One bartender remained, the Jesus-eyed man with a ginger beard who was promised pay but he never got the checks, week after week. He showed up for tips, and ran his own business on the side.

The bar would be closed some days, then mysteriously reopen. I was there in the winter. I came through the spring rains. I came in the summer months made of smog and burning foliage. I showed up like a walking-talking vagina yearning to be entered by the cock, the hands, the nature of this man. We laughed as the fluids took their effect. He was once a poet and he knew how to speak to me, make me shine.

The day came that the bar closed, and remained closed. The owner botched his "boardroom moment" by threatening to pistol-whip a cache of investors ready to renovate his dungeon of pinball and mirrored walls.

(...sugar-walls, cock-walls, fuck-me calls...)

There is a world of muscles and fast cars. It is a world of exertion, of women on hold, of bodies who charge for the promise of holding. I may be a tourist in this world, but only in the way I am a tourist in every world. I pass like gas, and stay alive.

Publix Hotel/Joe's

IN DOWNTOWN SEATTLE by Union Station there is a corroded metal awning that reads Publix Hotel, and at certain points the metal has corroded a micron wide, and at some points you could (if you were already levitating) hold your breath and ease right through it. As the clouds cover the sun and you gaze at the awning of the Publix Hotel, you get the feeling that you are standing in a three-dimensional daguerreotype. Within spitting distance of the awning is a cartoonish mural of Bruce Lee, and an endless stream of potato-shaped men in billowy gray T-shirts pose for camera-phone photos pretending they are engaging with Bruce in a battle to the death.

Within spitting distance (or perhaps we should say kicking distance) of Bruce is Joe's Bar. This is Chinatown, and the sidewalks feel supercharged with an endless flow of commuters, hobos, and darling cartoon-perfect Asian girls who wear knockoffs of supermodel finery. Their postures are so erect; their beauty is so embraced; their arms flail in the air with choreographed gestures of delight. For the rest of their lives they shall never be as alive as they are today, and it is our duty as spectators to savor them. They function as the circulation, the wind itself, and this wind passes over and purifies the grizzled pates of the patrons of Joe's Bar.

You cannot miss Joe's Bar. You cannot miss the neon in the windows, and the open doors, where men spill onto the sidewalk in rumpled raingear, wizard outfits, and all of those T-shirts that feature Joe Camel and choppers and American flags.

There is a jukebox playing in Joe's, and it is always playing.

In fact this is a cult of the jukebox, and the clientele, upon entering, innately understand it is their duty to feed the box, insure that music is always flowing, is honey, is manna, is wine in the air. When the music stops, you can hear a general muttering and a clapping of hands, but this relative silence will not do.

The tall black man is the Gatekeeper, and he strides a little sideways, and stands as long and thin as a voodoo icon in a navy windbreaker, Coke-bottle glasses, nondescript baseball cap, shuffle-shuffle over to the jukebox. He doesn't want to have to spend all his money, but it has to be done. The music must play.

Around his table is a parchment-faced woman with oily blonde hair, jeans, and battered T-shirt. She smacks her mouth back and forth and cries, "I want the Scorpions!" but it turns out that "Boogie Nights" is going on instead. A small elderly man who looks South American does soft-shoe in his cloud-gray attire. His clothing is pitifully forgettable; it is so gray compared to the life which keeps on dancing. A Native American woman gets up and shows off disco moves that slice through the air. Her hustle, her funky chicken, all of her assorted tricks and treasures are on display. As she is advancing in age, her limbs are stiff, and she moves with the jerkiness of an animatronic puppet, like the ones I saw as a child in Chuck E. Cheese.

My bandmate and I were in there for an hour or so, and we passed a series of tests. We sat long enough, we drank long enough; we bobbed our heads to the music, and soon the tall man in his baseball cap, the one I call the Gatekeeper, he came over and asked if I would select a song on the jukebox.

I felt like I was on the spot. He showed me his five-mile-wide smile. This, he told me, was my welcome to the bar. He escorted me to the box where I stared down at that glass pane, and I flipped through the pages of tepid fare like Foghat and Southern Rock compilations and a two-box Led Zeppelin set and Rod Stewart's Greatest Hits and Thriller. I unconsciously felt a pressure to pick something unexpected, something more soulful and yet unexpected than what was on display before me.

The song I picked never ended up going on while I was there.

The Gatekeeper beckoned me to his table with a sort of mythical whisper.

At first I wondered if he was saying, "Do you like penis? Penis?" But after approaching him where he sat magisterial with the heavy metal woman and the boogie night machine-dancer, I watched him remove an enormous bag of unshelled peanuts from his backpack and offer it to me.

First of all, I don't have the patience to shell unshelled peanuts. Secondly, the amount of peanuts in this bag would fill seven times the real estate of my stomach. His consorts grinned at me and said, "Awww honey, yuh donnnave to!"

I concurred. I said, "Ya know, I'm really glad you offered them but I'm just not gonna eat these."

I gave him my confidential face. My confidential face is a smile. And the Gatekeeper grinned, a sheepish grin. And he held out both of his hands and we did a complicated handshake and we both smiled and he said he just wanted to welcome me to the bar. And I felt very welcomed by this man so old with a crystal-river voice that rang in a duet with a jukebox Roy Orbison; this man, this ebony tower of smoke.

Right before we left, a second man with a brilliantined salt n' pepper quiff and a polo shirt and a louche disregarded body burned a crab shade offered us YET ANOTHER dollar to make selections....

The barflies drank. And cackled. And drank. And they made sure the music would never end, because when the music is over....

Little Snow Pants in the Face of Global Warming

IN TODAY'S PHONE CALL with my mother, she told me that the neighbor who usually mows her lawn isn't doing as good a job as usual because his wife has hundreds of nodules in her lungs and this is most likely a "distracting" situation. She said her other neighbor has cut down a lot of his trees, and whenever he leaves his house he appears "apprehensive of women"; however, I am imagining that the only way she could measure this, being a woman who stays inside her house most of the time, is if she accidentally happens to be getting the mail at the same time he is. She also told me that with the wind chill factored in, it is supposed to feel like forty below zero tonight, and that she doesn't know whether or not to drag her garbage bags to the curb. She said that the only places open today were churches, and the news is telling everyone to stay indoors. She says the wind in the branches keeps her awake at night. It whistles. It cries. She said that Boston is buried beneath snow, much worse than Syracuse.

She says, "This is the supposed to be the most severe winter on record."

I say, "Well, the weather is haywire because the polar ice caps are melting. This may be one of the last years that the human race experiences such severe cold. We are on the path to extinction. We have brought about environmental degradation so great, it is irreversible."

She says (without missing a beat): "Remember that blizzard when you were a little kid where the snow was over your head? You had your little snow pants on to keep warm and you were adorable in them. Your grandmother had to go to the hospital in the ice and I was marching you around the house in your little snow pants to keep warm. You were so adorable!"

In a nutshell, I think this is my mother's generation's answer to global warming.

Sunday Snow

I **WAS BORN ON THANKSGIVING** on the cusp of a paradigm shift, short-lived. I was born in the cradle of the seventies before the Nixon/Reagan corporate minions cracked down on every social program, before every last free-thinker was assassinated, jailed or discredited. I remember the colors and feelings of this time well. It LITERALLY WAS like being born in a rainbow nation. But I'm not writing about society today; I am writing about a maternity ward, and a baby named Sunday Snow.

It was Thanksgiving. My mother went into labor, and it was a difficult labor, twenty hours long. The maternity ward of Crouse Irving Memorial Hospital was packed. The streets were crusted in snow; doctors were reluctant to leave their family congregations and snifters of this and that to blearily drive back to the hospital.

The maternity ward was in an older wing of the hospital; the windows rattled with ice, and an Edwardian pallor was cast over the old gurneys and bedside tables and their glass pitchers of water. The nurses, mostly old Irish Sheela-na-gigs with Ratched bodies and mother-hen instincts, they patrolled the expectant mothers, many in severe distress. Ya see, the doctors were very reluctant to leave their family dinners, so there was literally a LINE of mothers in labor, trying, in essence, to hold it in, until the proper medical attention could arrive. For some reason I imagine the maternity ward to be as big as an orphanage and lit only by candles at night. This is how I prefer to imagine the circumstances of my birth.

My mother was lying there, a high-risk pregnancy. The deal was that being Rh-negative, her blood was not supposed to touch mine during the calisthenics of birth. In fact she ended up having a C-section; but this is many hours away. In the meantime, she watched the drama unfold with a baby named Sunday Snow.

There was a young hippie in the bed next to my mother, who apparently came from a good family, and she was having a baby out of wedlock (a big deal back then). Her parents crowded around the bed, feeling uneasy that the father was there—a stoned dude with long hair who started eating the mother's hospital-issue hot lunch right off her plate the minute it arrived.

The girl was trying to convince her parents that she wanted to name her baby Sunday Snow. As my mother told me this tale with a combination of revulsion and sympathy in her voice, I couldn't help but wonder where Sunday Snow is now.

Did her parents stay together longer than two weeks after her birth? Did Sunday actually get named Sunday Snow, or did the grandparents talk her mother out of it? I wonder what her last name was? Sunday Snow Guildenstern, perchance?

And what about the mother? Did she become a yuppie once the eighties hit and have Sunday's name legally changed to something like Brittany, so that Sunday could be admitted to a prestigious girls' school in Tenafly, New Jersey?

Sex and the City

THE REAL WOMEN WHO DRINK and dine and date like the figments of *Sex and the City* have faces like discarded wads of wax paper and they can barely walk because their bunions have swollen to the size of sumo wrestlers and those wrestlers are warming up for the big match in each scuffed ponyhair Louboutin, each scuff insuring the resale value of its respective pump is nil. Speaking of pumping, the middle lady pumps iron twice a day because she knows that from behind her sinewy physique can still pass for a twenty-year-old, and they clatter and they honk and the sound of each sole on the concrete feels like a sure and discrete murder.

Privates

AS A SMALL CHILD I was unfamiliar with the details of male anatomy. I had already been exposed to countless images of medieval Adams, their crocus-pale and usually Flemish loins covered in fig leaves; male ballerinas on PBS holiday specials like the *Nutcracker*, each lavender leotard impacted with arcane and mysterious knots. What was contained within? Balled-up newspaper? Freshly laundered socks?

I thought about these bulges, but didn't think for long. Television was instead devoted to the female form. By the age of five I was already deeply familiar with the notion of delicious breasts, the more fatty, the better; and I had decided in my infinite wisdom that I preferred women in harem garb—Busby Berkeley casts of maidens giving peekaboos from the shadows of pastel, floor-length veils; denizens of ancient Babylonia and Atlantis who never failed to resemble corn-fed blondes from Minnesota transformed by tanning lotion and gin rickeys into pleasure domes of myth. My ideal woman was Tina Louise from *Gilligan's Island* crossed with Rita Moreno. Sex sells, and it was sold to little girls to the point I may as well have been a lesbian.

Starting at the age of four, I stripped to my own reflection in the mirror, because I wanted to be like these beautiful women on teevee. And I should add that these stripteases aroused me at that age! Never underestimate the imaginations of wee ones.

But I digress! This is supposed to be about my discovery of the male form. My first exposure to it occurred when I was playing a game of hide-and-seek with my friend Helen. Her grandparents were Polish immigrants whose house was behind my grandparents' house.

I lived with my grandparents, but Helen only visited hers once every weekend. I was a serious misfit with toothpick legs and a desire to discuss Greek mythology with strangers. Helen was not a misfit; she understood the virtues of lip gloss and scented erasers. Since she was just visiting, she tolerated my uncool ways, and instead of being embarrassed by them, she was amused by them.

Helen's father was a lawyer and she lived in a wealthy part of town in one of those modern eighties box-houses—the sort that literally resembles a shoebox, and like a shoebox, is solely meant for the storage and display of novelty items. She was popular in school, and had four older brothers whose rooms were filled with laser-light displays and posters of women in bikinis, women who resembled chicken wings. The women in these posters were glazed, were tenderized, were very much like something one would find under heat lamps at a local buffet, and these soft-focus frails, like the *houris* promised to Persian assassins, fed their teenaged masters nightly.

Look at me! I have gotten back to the female form—because there is no escape!

Helen's grandparents were called Boppy and Jodge. They did not speak very much English. They lived in a simple brick house that reminded me of an exotic jail cell, filled with Catholic icons, austere wooden dressers, and the faint scent of mothballs. Their basement was filled with items from the fifties and sixties that they could not bear to dispose of. Like a lot of old Polish couples I saw back then, they were packrats extraordinaire. After all, who knew when those items would become useful again? I remember walking through aisles of cardboard boxes in the basement and feeling like an archaeologist, unearthing fox stoles with the little heads attached, and a leopard-print nylon robe smelling of mildew which I coveted like nobody's business.

Boppy and Jodge were fascinating, rumpled aliens to me. Boppy's breasts loomed huge beneath her cotton tops, and her hair was an anemic root beer color: frizzy, as if it could not accept a comb. Her face was lined by endless creases from laughter, and she dined on a rubbery red glob of cow liver several nights a week.

Jodge—he was the stoic one. Tall, made of sinew, his hair as white as a summer cloud. He wore rectangular wire-framed glasses and suspenders clamped to old-man pants. I had the feeling that even if he had the skill of fluent English, he would not speak very much.

One day Helen and I were playing hide-and-seek, and I had a brainstorm. I was all of six years old. I decided to creep into the bathroom and hide behind Boppy and Jodge's shower curtain.

Ten minutes passed...fifteen. Helen was probably eating popcorn and watching cable tee-vee in the other room, just leaving me hanging on purpose. She was a cool kid, and did things like that.

It was then that I heard footsteps approaching the bathroom door. My heartbeat raced. I concentrated on making my muscles rigid, my breathing controlled. I had to be very, very still.

When the sounds got nearer, I realized that it was not Helen entering the bathroom. The door shut, and the slow, grunting silences of an old man undoing his fly and pulling out his wee-wee commenced.

Jodge began to urinate, and at that point I think I must have made a motion, one which made Jodge shuffle backwards, and actually...start laughing. This man I had never seen even smile up to this point in time was so amused that he started laughing, and I started laughing, too.

I emerged from behind the shower curtain as he finished buckling his belt. I did not actually see his equipment—however I was able to watch his presence through the gauzy shower curtain and come to the conclusion that men stood up while urinating rather than sitting down, and that the process involved pulling something "out" of the genital region.

I was unclear on what resided in that region, or what shape it had, but I had been enlightened nevertheless.

A couple of years later I saw a five-year-old kid running around the neighborhood in a pair of shorts, and nothing else. He showed me his penis. I think he had a crush on me, and I wished he was older so I could do something about it. I was such a misfit that I didn't rule out the possibility of having to wait for the neighborhood toddlers to grow up, to have meaningful conversations with them about astrophysics and war.

Gettin' Busy

NOTHING SAYS SAINT PATRICK'S DAY like a blond wavy-haired stoner dude carrying a 36-pack "DELUXE" box of condoms and asking where the "Dry Shampoo" talcum powder is because he doesn't have time to wash before a big date. With these two details an entire narrative unfurls before my eyes...

Lone Rangers

I SPENT A YEAR IN FRANCE when I was eighteen years old. I lived with a "host family." I'm sure that some of you Americans are familiar with this practice. An American kid, usually a student, lives in another country, having to take classes and speak the language of the "foreign land" until she is lubricated, pummeled, turned into a side of Kobe beef by the alien rhythms of speech, fashion, touch and undress, to the point she could pass as a native—not quite.

When I was in France, I started living in a way that didn't jive with my host family. I stayed out all night almost every night with wannabe rock stars and psychedelic artists who lived in warehouses and read books by Patti Smith and asked me what the words meant. I started dating a guy with long dyed-black hair, though dating is such a subjective word in the end, wouldn't you say? You, even you in marriages, you whisper, you feel that all romance is subjective in the end.

We had sex. I rode on top of him under the influence of wine and vodka and incense-black bricks of hashish that felt warm to the touch like Nairobi hands. For a brief period of time, the man I was with moved into a squat, but most of the time he stayed in a room of his mother's duplex apartment on a street named after a general, where all the buildings were a squat putty-brown and the street signs were a navy blue. It could be France, or it could be a French colony like Cambodia, Vietnam.

I would tiptoe up and down the stairs of this duplex because Olivier did. That was his name. We would come in at any hour of the night and try to quietly eat something in his mother's kitchen, and Olivier would invest painstaking amounts of muscular reserves to tiptoe in just the right spots, open the refrigerator door at just the right speed, try not to knock over the chinoiserie umbrella stand despite being so wasted he could not utter words—only laugh with wet lips the color of a baby's nipple.

It was after months of successive visits to his mother's rooms that I came up with the vision in my mind of his mother being a sort of shrew who might whip him with words or banana peels if he so much as dropped a stray hair in the bathroom sink. In fact her home was so meticulously clean, I am certain that I could have blended tropical milkshakes in her toilet and I could have thrown them back in rapid succession with no ill effects.

From Olivier's stories, and from my observations of her cold, fluorescent-lit kitchen, I got the impression that this lady was a very isolated soul. She worked in an office somewhere, and when I did run into her, sometimes earlier in the evenings, she gave me a curt nod, and nervously pronounced "Bonjou—" and to a degree we were all quite civil, even though she clearly was disappointed in her son, out of work, always on drugs, with that crazy long dyed-black hair like a death-cult version of Elvis.

His eyes were a piercing blue; they could sear through mountaintops and chisel diamonds like a divine flame.

This woman, I do not remember her name. I could call her Helene, or Eloise, or Violette. She had precise lemon-colored hair that reminded me of sorbet. She, like her son, had a glacial quality to her physique.

There were no messes; there were no stains; there were no balls of lint on the floor, or beer cans behind the couch. In her refrigerator, a plastic honeybear was kept upside down so that this lady could utilize every last micro-managed ounce of its innards in her verveine tea.

Tea to sleep; tea to deliver peace. But how can one so isolated ever have peace? How can eight magazines precisely arranged and a street devoid of traffic deliver; and the hum of the refrigerator looms so loud at night, and the caress of a man is so remote, if it is even desired.

Yet tonight my own walls tower over me like the walls of Olivier's mother. My dishes are too clean. My blood beats too loudly. I cannot take this being alone for one moment in time. I want to break out of my body and crack open these walls and fly like a bird of death or disease or revolution over the rooftops and find something to fuse with, another bird of life or terror or joy.

Downtown Motorcyclebar

I AM SITTING IN A CORNY BAR full of dangling motorcycles and overinsulated ribs. I watch an office party gone bad, women who resemble rock formations ignore each other's childhood stories with farm squints and razor-thin smiles. I watch a woman in lumberjack clothes and a bleeding forehead make out with a boyfriend who looks like a child star gone wrong, gone feral. I watch a woman who could be my daughter give her friend her life history of tattoos. After the one on her ribs, her mamma didn't speak to her for two weeks. A man in a ski hat and a paisley vest prances around and I don't know why. He looks as fragile as a crystal swan. Three men dressed as Santa Claus get drunker, and at the very least they have a groupie also dressed in plush red polyester, a female Claus. The Keno women spend an hour here and retire. A pair of buttocks with Eartha Kitt's head lazily dances to her own reflection in a wall-mounted mirror. Five Dutch businessmen grope her loose pajama bottoms and decide on a price.

The Female Gollum

WHO SAID chivalry was dead?

The female Gollum is a schizoid speed freak who gives Nina Hagen a run for her money. It is amazing the voices and phrases this woman is generating. "Can I be a cunt? But can ya? Can ya?" "Titanium! Titanium!" "Yes. Yes Darlin,'" "Can ya a-taunt for einstein jean," "But can ya can ya can ya why not?" "Yes." "But canya canya canya whyna?" Very intricate rhythms, some which remind me of the indigenous music of Ghana...crossed with Elmer Fudd crossed with Nina Hagen and Yosemite Sam...are you getting the sonic picture yet? A laryngectomy rasp, or is her throat just worn out from all the projection? Her foot kicks in rhythm to the words, a sockless foot in a canvas sneaker. She wears a long black skirt with a glittery top that from this distance might be sequins or vinyl. Her hair is a ratted blonde mess like Courtney Love, her mouth is a gaping toothless hole, and her skin is white turned terra cotta from nonstop sun.

Two homeless men collecting bottles on bicycles come to her aid and offer her a pack of cigarettes and casual conversation. One guy is young with sunglasses and the other is a bearded man who is with age turning gray as the pavement. They are tender, and by their words they distract her, yank her out of her fugue. They speak to her as they would a child.

They ask, "What you been doing all day, drinkin'?" And talk to her about the buses, as she is at a bus stop. The traffic is so loud I don't hear it all. She has to enunciate extra-looooong for each word because she hardly has any voice left, it is just croaaaaaak, croaaaa-wuhky-crooooooak. All that remains is the gristle of a live-wire pirate, all supernova-sunburn-wildfire-mania black hole contagion. The bike-men finally part and wish her well and say "You keep that pack, honey." Now she has cigarettes to do something else with her mouth, and she is reminded that there is something better to humanity, not just the world that has haunted her in her head for who knows how long, the eternal and soul-eating cartoon.

Bus Hostage

I ROLLED INTO PORTLAND, spent from a summer-long camping trip with a couple of hippies who had not found their chosen gods in the Rockies, Sedona, or under the Golden Gate Bridge. They went back to New York, the Reality from whence we came, but I lingered in this foggy place.

I'm not kidding when I speak of fog. Portland is sealed under it from November to April. A black river cuts through the city like a dead eel. You move here and people tell you a myth: Local tribes believed the river valley captured spirit energy and wouldn't release it. For this reason no one settled its banks until the crazy-eyed pioneers came, filled with a yearning that thousands of miles of struggle made stranger than fiction.

I moved here and there were ghosts all right—of pipe-cleaner men in porn stores! There were more porn stores than toilets in this city. Every other block downtown had glittering signs advertising live nudie shows, glory-hole assembly lines. The Portland of 1995 was a twinkle in the eye of the Mecca it would one day become. It was a land of squinty pink faces, mushrooms, moss; a land of docks, trains, goose turds and steel.

I was twenty-two years old. I found a room with a Murphy bed. I worked at a magazine housed in a building shaped like a piece of cake. A coffeehouse and a vintage store were on the ground floor. The coffeehouse was considered one of the "hip" hangouts in town, where, at any given time of day, a person could walk in and get twenty head-to-toe stares from a hive of women with rainbow-colored hair, platform boots and fetish collars. I found the young men of the city to be far more bizarre than the women: Lean creatures with skin as thin as the coating of a goldfish, such that you could see their veins, and organs, and even last night's meal pass through those organs to its ultimate fate. These men had closely cropped hair that had not been washed for several generations. In fact the hair on these men's heads was older than the buildings they stood in, for it had not been washed, I think, since the dinosaurs roamed the earth.

I met a woman who was in love with one of these men, these fish-men in gas station attendant jackets, and shirts that were more hole than cotton-weave. She was an artist who drove around in a lemon-yellow Karmann Ghia. Her charcoal pastels embraced the curves of this man with a hunger that no one body could fulfill. I first saw him in her portraits, hanging on the wall of her Northwest apartment, his naked bones in poses of louche arousal near the closet where her shoes hung on a metal rack, so precise.

When I finally met him, I could not keep my eyes off his hair. I felt that any woman caressing him could actually LOSE herself inside the grease of his hair. It would start with a tender stroke, and—GLOP!—the whole arm might disappear up to the elbow! And then before she knew it, she might be wedged inside his adenoids, or perhaps lodged between two crenellations of his brain, like a cyst, like a buried twin.

When I think of my first months in Portland, I think of these Joey Ramones and dollfaces, these big little boys and girls listening to grunge and dressing in drag and doing cabaret and calling softcore photo shoots high art as if no one had thought of this before!

The magazine I worked at started out as a literary magazine, but as it expanded to have international fame, it featured interviews with pop stars, playwrights, performance artists. I would go to the office every day in what I felt was my "adult" attire—high-waisted skirts with satin blousons and vintage velvet jackets. My hair was peroxided as white as a moon rock. My face was covered in weeping sores. I carried myself, girded in stage makeup and combat boots, as if I was in some way an intellectual superior to the people I met "on the scene."

Of course underneath I was desperately lonely. I felt like a tourist. It was always raining. The sky was purple where the clouds would strafe the hills of ink-black spruce trees, a forest that threatened to encroach on the city like a tidal wave. "Downtown" was twelve blocks wide—barely larger than a postage stamp!

I would leave the office where I had reworked an interview with a friend of Keith Richards, or an artist who made clothing out of tampons, or a group of girls who dressed as babies and sang songs about woman power, and I would see those same faces—always the same faces!—installed like living art in front of the café's windows, pouring in more coffee to wake for the lives they led at night. At moments I wondered if the entire valley was under a sleeping spell.

One of my favorite things to do in a new city was to take the public transit to places I didn't know about. I'd walk over bridges. I'd go in bars and cafés. I'd float through the supermarkets and strip malls and let the conversation wash over me as if I was a lizard, and the human race was a sun I needed to bask in.

Heading south of Portland, you see things turn desperate, and fast. You see boulevards lined with pawn shops, Korean grocery markets and Mexican taquerias; decaying houses with bright pastel signs out front advertising "LIVE Lingerie Models Inside." There are a lot of lingerie models on 82nd Avenue, the street that leads to Clackamas Town Center, a mall where I went every weekend to watch meth-heads and amoebic families shop for gadgets and curtains to hang on their flesh.

This mall had some bizarre stores, like one where you could "Design-A-Bear"—stuffed animals that were supposed to be "built" right in front of a kid; personalized nightmares so invasive in their "cuteness" that I imagined each bear as being remote-controlled by a pedophile. I remember a photo booth where a buck-toothed metalhead kept trying to get me to pose for "free photos." I remember a frizz-headed granny who liked my go-go boots. I remember sugar—a veritable Niagara of sugar being poured via pink, purple and sunset-colored fluids into the gullets of thousands of people who, with pyramids of molested fast-food wrappers in front of them, now slumped, spent in their plastic seats, and having consumed the food, they resembled the piles of litter spread before them far more than they were recognizable as human beings. The offspring of these families, the young ones, the firm, those covered in dew and drugstore perfumes, these youths would be on the ice rink strutting their stuff, gliding with an ease that seemed to come from a knowledge deep within that this would be the best time they would ever have in their lives before turning into their parents.

There were more "urban," or prosperous, malls I could go to—and I did—however the people in Clackamas Town Center were the most interesting to me, perhaps because they were uniquely Oregonian. These were the descendants of the trappers and loggers and cowboys who settled this land and put the final brushstrokes on the great genocide we affectionately call the settling of the Old West.

In Clackamas Town Center, you'd see emaciated seniors—the Tammies and Bambis of yesteryear—in hot pink lipstick and leopard-print halter tops, with no teeth. You'd see entire families of men in overalls and expressionless faces eating popcorn with tins of chewing tobacco resting by their wrists. You'd see goth kids, timid and clinging to each other in groups of two or four, testing out inventive uses of hair gel and Sharpie fake tattoos. This was the strutting-place of buzzards who were in no way legitimized by whatever happened in "The City"—a city which, even though it was just a twenty-minute bus ride away, sounded, in the words of these elders, like it might be as far away as "Communist Russia."

"That's where colored people urrr," you'd hear them mumble, "I don't feel safe." Growing up on the East Coast, I could assure these bunker-dwellers that they had no idea how small the numbers of black people were in their conservative state.

One afternoon I got on the wrong bus, thinking that it went to my favorite shopping mall. Instead it took me to the dying forest, to the mold-festooned bathrooms and child feet kicking and kicking and never giving in beneath and between and inside these jittery wraiths.

49

It was the dead of winter. It was four in the afternoon. The sun had already set. I got on downtown with a number of rush-hour commuters, and in twenty minutes we were easing down 82nd, close to where I figured the mall was—but the bus went further. It turned on a highway I didn't recognize, and soon it was cruising down suburban streets, making rights and lefts in a neighborhood of small houses and trailer homes.

The crowd of people who had been on the bus were depleting fast. At the final stop, a woman in a puffer jacket and nurse's scrubs, her face a jaundiced yellow under the bus lights, shuffled down the steps, leaving only the driver and myself.

He parked the bus. This was an unorthodox situation.

It was, as the song goes, "just the two of us."

The thought raced through my head: Does he wonder why I am still sitting there? Why I didn't get off at a stop? Does he think I'm staying on here...for HIM?

We were at the terminus, the inevitable end of every bus line where a driver has a piss and a smoke, consulting his or her watch for the correct time to turn on the ignition and return to the route. This is normal.

At first glance, the driver appeared to be normal. He was in his late thirties. He had the build of a former athlete. Lean muscle adhered to bones as long as hockey sticks. His face and neck were crab-color from days spent under the sun. His hair was short, mildly spiked with gel, not unusual for the year 1996.

I watched as the driver got out of his perch, stretched his arms in the air, and he slowly, as if he was following a military procedure, removed a folded newspaper from a storage area behind his seat. He swaggered to the handicapped seats, lowered his body and started leafing through the paper.

I was seated halfway back, not too close to the front, but close enough that I felt the need to "look busy." In my bag I had a folder of writing to proof. I could use my stack of papers as an excuse, a way to not be "available" to the driver.

For a time, this worked. Three minutes passed. Five...seven...

How long were we going to BE there?

I noticed the driver peer up from his newspaper once and a while. He noticed me—but of course he did! What age did I look? Eighteen? Twenty? I gave a neutral yet friendly head-nod, the sort people give each other in bars and at traffic lights, as if to indicate: Still alive? Yep, still alive.

Carefully and slowly, as if he were going through a drill, the driver refolded his newspaper and tucked it into the spot behind his seat. He returned to the wheel.

A sigh of relief went through my body. YES! He is going to turn the bus back on and we can just get out of this uncomfortable situation!

He turned the ignition. He killed the interior lights. The joyride began—or should I call it a painride?

The bus veered out of the suburb. It started racing down country roads. With the interior lights off, it would appear that the bus was off-duty. I could see that we were no longer on the route that had led to the terminus.

The bus was traveling on roads so remote that I didn't see houses, or even streetlamps. The driver made his bus lurch over bumps. Its sides began to rattle in a strange way. He steered his tonnage with a frenzy that made me think of Paul Revere galloping on his horse, the Revolutionary War as told to us in ancient grade school textbooks:

Stallions! Lanterns! Bells of blood and invasion! Watch out, kiddies, a bayonet will floss your guts for good! Listen children, and you shall hear of the bus driver's brain that went very queer...

I decided to stay in my seat, see if an out would present itself.

"Come on up!" The driver said, "I won't bite..."

I stress, THIS WAS NOT AN OUT.

I wondered if I should ask where the bus driver was going, but I thought better of it. I waited a minute, gathering my bag, my body in slow motion.

"Hey, really, I'm not gonna bite 'cha."

I could hear in his words the same swagger as his walk. The role was playing the man.

Step by step, I moved to the front of the bus, gripping each seat as the vehicle swerved through ink-black night.

We were entering the forest that stood tall and dark in a soil full of termites and wriggling worms—a cold world, beyond the hum of farms. It felt like we were increasing in elevation. I plopped my butt in one of the handicapped seats behind the driver's chair.

I am not a delicate flower. Well maybe I am, but I have found ways to push through my "package" in favor of experience. By this point I'd camped on city blocks as comfortably as I camped in the woods, or on the floors of strangers I'd met at last call. I felt that I could "work with" almost any situation, but I wasn't a fool. I knew that I had to approach each madman with caution, especially one in control of twelve tons of bus.

The engine was straining to climb a mountain road. The driver shifted gears and whistled at the windshield. He began to shuffle, haphazard, through a videotape in his mind:

"You know this used to be beautiful country, before all the Mexicans showed up. They took our jobs. We didn't know that was going to happen when we were kids. The whole country was different when we were kids."

Is that so? I thought to myself, but I just let him ramble.

"When I was a teenager, my friends and I, we thought we were studs. We thought we were gonna get jobs in logging or take over our family farms, but the economy is ruined now and the jobs just aren't there, and it's because of Bill Clinton and all of his Democrat cronies in Washington! They sold this country to the Chinese, let the Mexicans in...you know you can't even order FOOD without having to repeat what the goddamn words are five hundred times? These fucked-up Mexicans are breeding all over the place, they have five, ten kids each family. Soon they will outnumber us and there won't be anyone left to RUN this country!"

His glassy eyes fixed on me—a look meant to tell me that he was an ancient man, a man of a past I couldn't begin to understand.

"It wasn't like that at all when I was a boy." He leered at me, "We had FUN! Me and my buddies, we'd drive up to Mount Hood and we'd smoke grass and we'd swim in the creeks and you know what I mean? We had chicks, a lot of chicks, and we had the TIME OF OUR LIVES. Kids can't do that anymore. They have to worry if they're gonna have jobs at all because THE MEXICANS ARE TAKING OVER!"

He zigzagged back and forth: Happy-sad, happy-sad.

"You know I still snowboard in the winter, but nothing's the same! We used to look forward to a future then, but I don't know where this country is going now...run by Ivory Tower liberals not lookin' out for the little guys like me. Don't give a FUCK about little guys like me!"

"Theirs is a kind of wealth," I said, "that is beyond our imagining."

"It's a wealth made of MY sweat, my buddies' sweat! Ivory Tower liberals don't give a DAMN who they sell out! There used to be logging here. That wood was used in the U-S-A. You know where all that wood goes now? Guess. Guess..."

"Mexico?"

"It goes to fuckin' Japan! FUCK Japan! They're like the Trojan Horse, smiling and pretending to be good guys, and they'll sell us all their crappy cars and bow with their slanty eyes until it's time to stick it in!"

Stick it in where? I thought to myself.

"You think you can trust anyone? Well?" he eyeballed me, "You can't..."

"You probably can't," I said to the homicidal bus driver.

The circumnavigations of the driver's mind made me think of that movie, *Network*, from the seventies. There's the anchorman who goes on national tee-vee and has a nervous breakdown. He starts screaming, "I'm mad as hell and I'm not going to take it anymore!" and it becomes a trend. Soon everyone all over the country is just cracking open, screaming in doctor's offices and supermarkets: "I'M MAD AS HELL AND I'M NOT GOING TO TAKE IT ANYMORE!" I felt like I was trapped in the middle of this driver's moment to crack, and what would become of us both?

I didn't have to wait too long to find out. The darkened bus sped along forest roads for another ten minutes, the driver giving what sounded like memorized speeches from AM talk-radio shows, until we entered farmland again.

Gas stations, diners, and feedlots appeared. I saw yards with propane tanks lined up like prehistoric eggs, gleaming gray, frost-covered in the dark. There were trailer parks, and no matter what they contained, friend or foe, there were people in those boxes—the warm, lamp-lit bodies of people.

The bus slowed. We were passing a strip mall and stopping at a traffic light. The driver hadn't shut his mouth for at least half an hour. At this point, he was spun out, a nervous system without skin. If a cartoon was to be made of the guy, he'd have foam leaking out of his mouth and coating the steering wheel, thousands of miniature bubbles slowly popping, each one reflecting the bloodshot eyes, the bloodshot skin and the dry flapping tongue of the driver.

"Did you know a MILLION sex crimes a year are committed by these Rico Suave fuckers? They're cockroaches! We should have exterminated them long ago!"

The bus was slowing at another intersection. The driver turned the lights on, but he wouldn't stop ranting. He pulled over to his first commuter stop, and a teenaged boy and two middle-aged women got on.

"It makes me wanna puke! It makes me wanna..."

The bus entered the city limits. I remained where I was seated in the handicapped seats, but now there were people sitting beside me and in front of me. The problem—well, one of them—was this:

The driver was still turning his head to me, directing every sentence at my face. As passengers got on, they gave ME confused looks, as if to say, silently: "You know this man? What is wrong with him? Are we going to get killed? Will I at least be driven to my stop so that you can stay on and get killed but I don't have to think about it?"

"It is not just our right, but our OBLIGATION to remove these atheist DICTATORS from power...because our once-proud country is becoming a BANANA REPUBLIC!"

Relief is too mild a word for the feeling I had as the bus crossed the Hawthorne Bridge and sailed downtown. I would be able to get off two blocks from where I lived. It was 7 p.m. The last dregs of rush-hour commuters were eager to press on and travel to the farthest reaches of the city, into sleepy suburbs and darkened streets that felt like sleep, like the leaking of gas from a pipe that slowly kills.

As I removed myself from the bus, I gave a final look at the driver, saying feebly: "I wish you luck in your endeavors."

His eyes were so wild, so spent, that I realized he wasn't registering my words. I couldn't tell if I saw something that resembled shame, or if it was simply exhaustion.

Later I did my research. The town at the terminus—the dark and silent block of trailers where I had watched the driver read his paper—is named Estacada. It sits thirty miles outside of the city, at the base of the Mount Hood National Forest.

Who knows what roads the driver and I traversed beyond the town on that mythic black-blood eve? Perhaps we left modern civilization altogether, and briefly went back to 1975, 1980, to an America that Ivory Tower liberals served cold and full of maggots to the Japanese, or the Mexicans, or maybe those "ex"-Soviets, too—THIS MAN'S GOLDEN YEARS, cooling, like the severed head of John the Baptist, a stream of Skoal juice partially dribbling from its mouth and forming an "au jus" halo on a silver platter.

I tell you, I never rode that route again. My tour of Estacada was done.

Toilet-Humper

THIS IS WHAT HE DID. It is not meant as a bizarre metaphor. The man would unzip his fly, shrug down his pants (or if he was in an elaborate mood, put on a ladies' slip) and straddle the toilet as if he was a woman and the cool porcelain contours bolted to the floor were the hips of a man.

The lid was up, exposing the placid bowl of water within, the target water. He would make a little tent for his cock with the palms of his hands and rub it against the seat. It looked like a balancing act, this making love, in a sense, to the entire waterworks of Portland, Oregon. He could be worshipping Poseidon or any number of ancient river nymphs with each slow-motion thrust.

What it really amounted to was a toilet seat, a not particularly clean toilet seat. Any seat would do.

When I first met him I was twenty-three years old and full of raging hormones, like some sort of salt-and-sugar-injected fast food that can only be purchased in dollar stores—but over the three years we dated, we grew apart, and I wouldn't always want to DO IT with him, which is when he would stroll to my bathroom with his enormous mop of hair on his unnaturally small face, a ratio that reminded me of a giraffe or some sort of prairie animal—and he would start GRINDING against the seat, with a method he must have perfected over time, because any RANK AMATEUR would have slid right off and fallen on his ass—and he would gaze at me, his moon-pale Welsh eyes bugging and then squinting, lips sucked inwards, brow furrowed in concentration, with each—slow—motion—thrust:

To find myself stared at by a person engaged in such an act, as if in his mind he was FUSING the image of my body to the sensation of the cold, smooth toilet seat—made me feel the impulse to laugh, but he was DEADLY SERIOUS.

He did not joke about this activity, or even smile when it was taking place.

Poseidon demanded the milk of his loins. Poseidon was in the sewer. Poseidon was beside himself.

Milky Way

OKAY, ONE MORE STORY about my friend Nicole in Rochester. You
see, even though she called her junkie-friends "vampiric," she wanted a taste. Hey, we both loved Lou Reed, you see? Both she and I
were twenty years old. We were hopeless misfits. I had smoked so
much hash by that point that I never wanted to be near it again. The
folks I knew who had harder drugs were into their own highs and
minds, had no interest in sharing with me. Penny-pinching skinflint
addicts, yeah! What other kind are there? So Nicole one night said,
let's get some heroin, and she did not call it by any slang names. She
ended up talking to two guys who would never have talked to me,
and they said they'd help her. You see, these guys looked like dumb
linebackers with hair the color of corn husks and muscles that went
on for miles. They talked to Nicole coz she was blonde and didn't
wear makeup, whereas I was walking around with black lipstick and
blue hair and I had the sort of body that was popular in New York
City, but not Rochester. No titties, man.

I felt that the linebackers would mess things up. They were just
too nervous. They pranced like cartoon roosters, like that Southern
General rooster that is in the Warner Brothers cartoons, Foghorn
Leghorn! The dudes didn't want to be a part of this operation so
much for Nicole and me; but they DID WANT DRUGS, and I suppose they felt a safety in numbers, a safety in this weird girl's car,
Nicole's car that we drove across the Genesee River and into the fall-
ing-apart blocks of pure poverty that girded the edge of the campus
like a black tidal wave being kept out by a dam.

As we got closer to the address that SOMEONE had acquired, the dudes in the front seat told us we should squat down in the back seat so that no one on the streets would see there were women left alone in the car. I remember feeling that the whole thing was idiotic. I craved the curried foods sold in corner stalls. I'd lived in Baltimore, London, and New York City by this point, and I didn't feel the fear of blackness that my companions had; yet I squatted with Nicole in the back seat anyway. I had a crush on her, and took the opportunity to lay my head near hers and see how she would respond.

After ten minutes, the blond dudes sauntered out of the building saying it was okay if we come on in. When we did, we went up a carpeted stairwell that smelled like urine and feet, in what was once a stately house now divided into rinky-dink rooms colored only by the unearthly spooge of tee-vee.

A family was in there. A guy and his girlfriend and a couple kids. There were some chairs, clothes thrown around, very little in the way of belongings. Two black men joined the two white men around the oven, an oven where something they were trying to do was taking a long time. They were heating up pouches of tinfoil over the oven's glowing orange radiator coils. A bare bulb over the oven showed me their faces, the little dances each man did in anticipation of the high. I saw bubbling white chunks on each tinfoil scrap. It looked like candy. The men proceeded to smoke this stuff out of pipes. Nicole decided to join them, wanting any experience, but I felt wrong "watching" the whole thing. One kid was asleep on the couch, and in another room, a very small room, like a closet, a baby was wrapped in blankets on the bed.

It was a small baby, maybe five or eight months old. The baby didn't have a crib. I wondered how often the baby rolled off the mattress, or if the baby was used to sitting there, wrapped up in swaddling clothes indefinitely. No light was on in the room; there was only a black-and-white tee-vee and it cast a blue glow over the baby's big eyes. I heard everyone's nervous chatter around the oven, and I sat down on the bed.

I stared into the eyes of this baby, wondering what it might be feeling. I just wanted to be there, for five minutes, ten, half an hour of forever with the baby. I muttered some gentle things to it, but didn't pick it up.

This wasn't my world, my place for picking up a baby I'd never see again. That baby's eyes were so big in the tee-vee light; that baby's eyes were as big as the Milky Way.

Tanked

THE WOMAN IN THE BAR where aging rock stars hide their guts is known as a party girl with her Tank Girl clothes and her stocking caps and beauty marks and hydrangea essential oil pits. She has Marilyn Monroe lips and widely spaced eyes like those of a goldfish, and for these reasons she is forgiven anything, even as she pulls down the baggy T-shirt meant to hide the drinking weight, and she thrusts her head in her hands and gives sweaty embraces to people she barely knows, and the man she is with looks like a robot longshoreman and she wants him so bad, and leans into his space, but he is acting aloof, nearly gay in his nonchalance. He has magician eyebrows. His eyes settle on me for a moment, detecting, adding up invisible volumes. His eyes are like flies, like laser beams. Blood turns to syrup in this room, closing the eyelids, making every mouth a vista to kiss. Who knew the inside of a man's mouth could feel five miles wide? These discoveries happen after the men sober up, grow placid, I find ground to hold my feet. My tongue cannot begin to comprehend the space.

Joplin/Japanese Doll

AT 10:30 A.M. THE ONLY PEOPLE on the bus are elderly people in motorized scooters and various potato-shaped middle-aged women who look like Janis Joplin and men who look like a series of dissolute Rick James impersonators in free-box clothes. As the bus picks up a new load at each stop, I start to get the feeling that I am not in a fully functional city so much as an amusement park made of methadone clinics and community gardens where the flotsam that spill out of the methadone clinics ease into the peaty shadows under rosebushes and sun their scalps after getting their morning's dose.

In such a reverie, I was on the bus headed up the hill when an elderly Japanese woman got on, and she had been sculpted by a master puppeteer; say Henson and Froud got together during the making of *The Dark Crystal* and decided that a little beyond the Skeksis Castle, there would be an old folks' home of delicate Japanese octogenarians who wear perfectly laundered Escada and vintage Kenzo silk blousons with Pierrot motifs.

For this is what this elder gentlewoman was going for: Her hair was in a transparent helmet, the sort of white hair that is dyed black but the black doesn't quite take and the entire helmet is a color somewhere between a sable brown and puce. Her blouse was a stark black silk featuring bold, palm-wide white circles and offbeat shapes that inhabited a realm between the not-quite circles and triangles. A conservative yet opulent belt showcased her waist, and beneath this were loose linen capris. On her feet were tasteful yet nondescript tan sandals. She was held in a column of air, not by strings, but by her own indomitable and terribly dignified spirit.

Her eyes registered alarm as she scanned the inhabitants of the bus. When her eyes settled on me, they relaxed somewhat. I was the only other person "dressed up" in anything resembling City attire. What city? It hardly matters what city! City is progress; city is cleanliness; city is the option, the privilege that one pays to be left alone.

Her sense of relief at scanning and assessing the value of my cosmetics and clothing was somewhat interrupted when she saw that I was hauling an enormous suitcase around. Women who look like me and carry suitcases—that usually means trouble. Am I some sort of battered woman escaping a tragic home? Am I a stripper or escort with a battery of costumes on hand to subjugate men made of hippo tongue within a ten-mile radius?

Whatever my imagined troubles were, this lady averted her eyes from the suitcase, clenched her cane, and attempted to lean on a metal bar near the bus driver's personal space. All seats were filled. I was standing, myself. There were simply TOO MANY handicapped or otherwise zombified people on the bus to avail a seat to her.

But then—that's when it happened! In front of me was a homeless-looking black man and a druggie-looking Janis Joplin woman and she was leaning into him with the casual "life is a party" mannerisms such women give to almost anyone who looks like he or she has some TIME.

And Joplin, she waved her pocked big arm at the Japanese woman and said, "Hey, there's a seat heer! Want my seat????"

Another look of quickly concealed panic: The elderly Japanese woman nodded a little of yes and a little of no and said, "No, thank you" with a puppet's smile.

The bus cruised on, and I thought of how the elder puppet was clearly not comfortable leaning on the metal bar but there were too many possibly sticky unknowns involved with taking the seat she was offered.

So I listened, as Joplin and her temporary companion spoke about life and the cosmos. And they did, I am not joking.

The black man was in his mid-forties, or so I gathered by his amount of gray hair, and he had a face that reminded me of a child; it had not been sculpted into the furrows of worry and bitterness you see in most people his age. There was despair, there was loneliness in that face, with his enormous lidded eyes that reminded me of those of a frog, yet his voice was stunted in the monologue of a child.

He did not originally come from Portland but had a brother who lived here. At one point in this man's life he had a dream or a vision; it was like a flash of light in his head that told him he had to come to Portland. "And so I did. Just like that. It has been hard, but I know God is taking care of me."

The man was simple, clinically simple. Older women had probably taken care of him his entire life, but now they were too old and he was too old. He was adrift, navigating the Earth by the gentle light cast by a celestial host of seraphim; angel choirs in azure-blue robes, clapping hands and playing lyres made of a crystalline sap, or so I imagine.

"I just believe God is taking care of me..." he went on. "Do you feel that way?"

"Well..." the fussy Joplin said, and I could imagine her when she was young, in spray-on denim flares and a short tough haircut looking like a member of the Runaways, smokin' in the girls room and cruising in bumblebee-yellow convertibles of dudes who called her a "Grade-A Stone Cold Fox."

This is where so many Stone Cold Foxes end up, and I love them for it. I could literally lick the face of every middle-aged Joplin Stone Cold Fox the way Mary Magdalene cleansed the feet of Jesus with her hair and spit and tears.

And Joplin said, "Well...I don't really believe in a guy in the sky, a God like that...but ya know...I think there's somethin', some kinda force around...I mean, there just HAS to be."

And I thought of how many people who ever lived on planet Earth decided there just HAD to be a force holding them in a loose embrace, not really loving them very much, but at least holding them, so the Earth wouldn't lose its gravity, so they wouldn't just fall off and drift like lost astronauts into a dark abyss of outer space. And that's when I saw a very tiny man, an elderly man who was as small as the elderly Japanese woman; he was so elderly that he wore loafers and a cardigan sweater and a tweed cap that made the back of his skull appear to be the size of a peanut, and his neck was as thin and wizened as a pretzel left forlorn to rot on a Ferris wheel. This old man slowly, woodenly gripped a guardrail and rose to his feet, calling to the Japanese woman and inviting her to take his seat. I think the seat was next to a young blonde woman, perhaps a college student—someone who looked like a "safe seating companion" on this bus of adversity.

And the old Japanese woman—she accepted this offer with a smile. Once she was seated, I caught her peering at me once, twice, three times, and realized that one doll was assessing another doll; someone carrying on the doll-Pierrot-mannequin tradition.

This pleased me. What she didn't know is that in my heart when I measure my composition, I am fifty percent Joplin bus troll and fifty percent elderly octogenarian doll and my soul, my birdlike fluttering sense of awareness keeps flying back and forth and perching on each identity, and feeling she is one, and then another, and then back to the first, and then I am elsewhere.

I am myth and inhabit a zone of myths. And then I am dislocated like a bone, like one of those seraphim who slipped off a cloud, like the astronaut unmoored, like the Joplin without a paper Dixie cup; like a Stone Cold Fox without a breast or a tight denim rear... dislocated in our molecular play.

Strippingest Stripper

I JUST SAW THE STRIPPINGEST STRIPPER I've ever seen just cross the street, presumably to strip on the other side.

If you want to know what the strippingest stripper looks like, I'll tell you: White hair so fried it spikes over her shoulders with the inability to accept a comb (this stuff would eat a comb like Cookie Monster eats chocolate chips), arm and leg tattoos, a bra used as a top, frayed spandex yoga shorts, flip-flops, and a shoulder bag overpacked with what may be a week's worth of hair and body-care essentials as she moves from couch to couch of friends' pads where videos of alien autopsies and eel sex are routinely played. And her face?? Her face is that of an Irish pixie left out for eight years in the desert sun. Her pot of gold took her to another dimension.

Running with Scissors

I JUST CAUGHT MYSELF RUNNING with scissors, and stopped myself. I am reminded of a friend who was cleaning out her ear with a Q-tip and she was so stoned that she answered the phone on an impulse, completely forgetting that the Q-tip was still inside her ear. She ruptured her eardrum and had to go to the emergency room. I was twenty-four when I knew her. She was thirty-two, an age so far ahead of mine that I viewed her as I now view elderly people, marveling at their dexterity and their sheer ability to keep moving their bodies through space, as if they have found new reasons to live each continuing day.

This said, she didn't look thirty-two at all. She had the dew of a teen. She was coated in tattoos before it was an everyday occurrence for soccer moms and bored teens. She had black Bettie Page hair, a collection of several leopard-print coats, and a huge portrait she had painted of Nick Cave which hung above her dim *Twin Peaks*-looking furniture sets. Her rented house reminded me of a voluptuous mortuary. All darkness, all mirrors; nothing to comfort a soul. I lost touch with her and heard that she had left town. At some point, like it happens with many hip chicas, she returned to the Portland vortex. We aren't able to stay away long.

I was at a glam rock show that was taking place in a gallery. Hundreds of art objects were being auctioned off for charities. The band came on and I suddenly recognized her profile in the crowd. She was doing something of a Crystal-Gayle-meets-Barbara-Mandrell heavily ironic seventies country star look, complete with a flower tucked behind her ear, offsetting her jet-black hair and China-blue eyes; the type of complexion so translucent that it is called "peaches and cream." What the flower didn't quite offset, though perhaps in a Nathaniel-Hawthorne-tragic-heroine-way, were the tears that were pouring down her lovely and skeletal cheeks.

She was the type of lady who dated junkies and rock stars, runners-up for Nick Cave. Who was she crying for? A dead pet, or a dying boyfriend? It HAD to be a man. I just sensed that if she was going to cry over something in public, it would be a man. Which man? Which drug or woman was he with instead of this pellucid rose?

I wonder where she is now. Is she running with scissors? I can't imagine her living life any other way.

Doe a Deer

I WAS ON A CROWDED BUS at rush hour and overheard a conversation between a lesbian and two heterosexual shopper-marms on their way home from a downtown outing. They were commenting to her on the large horn-like protuberances exploding from her stretched earlobes. These earplugs had limbs like tree branches, like something from an alternate universe that had unwittingly, by a subatomic glitch, gotten lodged in a woman's ears. The lesbian told her impromptu audience that the earplugs often snagged on the pubic hair of lovers she went down on, to the point that they would nurse cuts and abrasions afterwards. The middle-aged mavens cooed, "My goodness!" and the conversation dried out like an earlobe transported, by a subatomic glitch, to the surface of the moon.

Whack-Whack

IN ANOTHER LIFE she would have been Joan of Arc, but on this bus she was more like Nurse Ratched, the big blonde woman with arms like a titan who kept growling at her son and going whack! whack! with that pale pink hand against his cheek, his shoulder, his leg. I could hear her whacks impact his skin halfway back on the bus. It was rush hour and the bus was packed, and all of us heard the whacks, but none of us did anything, because we are civilized people.

Her face was very noble and very French, and her body was like a massive white temple, white flesh sheathed in a white cotton sundress and the whites of her eyes were aimed at a Kindle she held as if it was a crucifix. She held onto this little digital screen for dear life, as her son grabbed at her and begged for attention and she went "NO!" "SHUDDUP!" "Not NOW!" and whacked, and put his tiny neck in a headlock with that huge white arm that went on forever, an ocean of flesh.

The boy looked two years old and he had curly brown hair and Bambi-brown eyes and when she whacked him he would cry and this forced her to have to whack him again to shut him up and he wouldn't shut up, he would struggle to get off his seat and gaze at and touch the backpacks of strangers.

At one point he stopped crying because the bus was going over a bridge. The sight of flying, literally flying above a river and over an island made this child smile and look at the faraway glowing green trees with wonder. He stuck his arm out the open window and stared at the imprints of his fingertips on the glass and I could feel his feeling of magic, the magic of optics, the Oz-like apparitions of glass when you first discover them. But the glass and the island did not hold his attention for long. He tugged at the woman again, and she whacked him, and her eyebrows quivered, and she held that Kindle even tighter, brought it closer to her eyes as if she was doing a performance of reading for a most critical audience.

At this point an old lady got on the bus. Not elderly-old, more like in her late sixties, wearing a straw hat and white capris and sandals, in a look so many old ladies do which I call "Beachcomber Chic."

Instantly this old lady glommed onto the kid, sat right next to him, and started talking to the mother in that way that old ladies have when they want to reminisce about the joys of a motherhood they shall never experience again.

And the angry blonde...she actually picked up the boy and held him in her arms with a strange look of resignation, and started caressing him, and patting his bottom, and tenderly stroking his hair and kissing him on the forehead. She enveloped him in her endless flesh, her flesh like a parachute, the lining of a coffin; a late-spring rose. The look on her face was so bizarre, as if she had a distaste for doing this but she HAD to; it was ultimately the only thing that would quiet the boy.

And here was this old lady who had just gotten on and never saw the whacks, and we, the rush-hour bus people looking on in discomfort but feeling we could not change anything—and the old lady in her beachcomber attire was BEAMING with delight at having found this model young mother who was holding her baby just like a nativity scene.

The young mother smiled, and the old lady smiled, and I had to wonder what the mother was feeling underneath it all; would she one day lock this kid in a freezer and throw him off a bridge?

Oh sweet baby Jesus, what will this child remember of the big blonde when he is an old man, when he wears beachcomber chic in the year three thousand?

Womanly Hips Dog Man

A MAN WITH SAGGING JEANS on his womanly hips is briskly walking in the rain with a small white dog in his arms. The dog's head bobs in the air with each step, eyes like glistening coffee beans in a knuckle-white fur. The dog is cradled and re-cradled in the man's arms! This man cannot make enough adjustments to protect his baby. The dog wears a yellow vinyl raincoat, but it will never be enough. This man and his dog should live in a miniature model of the Mir space station.

Joyce DeWitt

FLASHBACK: I AM TWENTY-THREE YEARS OLD. I work at a punk club in downtown Portland making burritos for kewpie-doll children and tweakers and squatters and SSI cases. I am terrible at frying hash browns, and I come home every day covered in inches of grease. The woman who runs the club has agreed, for a fee, to be a certified caregiver for a dying ex-boyfriend. He is a junkie who is now, after years of drug abuse, having his body fall apart. He is losing toes and fingers to diabetes faster than a stripper loses G-strings and wads of ones before the sun doth rise. This man can't be more than fifty-three but he is as frail as an elderly crow, and he hobbles about with a cane and a Victorian dressing gown and a thousand-yard stare. He is a living corpse.

The woman hires us, her acquaintances and friends and art associates, to help move this guy's crap out of her house. His parents—looking far more vital than he does—a cheery Santa Claus and Mrs. Claus, rosy cheeks and Winston Churchill stiff-upper-lip cheer, are paying for this move, and for an apartment, this man's FINAL apartment in a brick building downtown, where he can die with dignity, out of the hair of the woman who slaved for him too long. Many a time I would visit her and see him throw cups of strawberry yogurt on the floor like a petulant child, like a man who once was a junkie.

We are huffing and puffing, struggling to get this guy's belongings into a super-duper deluxe-size U-Haul—but the hoard is never-ending! There are boxes of toys, and twine—one entirely filled with G.I. Joes—another one full of Fisher-Price plastic models of

73

playgrounds and schools—and a box full of cereal boxes!—and another box full of fabric scraps!—the junk is moderately interesting, but at this point in time, it feels useless. What is the dying man going to do now? Is he going to make some sort of sculpture or performance art with all of this JUNK NOW? The only item I really take a shining to is a homemade poster of Joyce DeWitt in her "rocker" phase—yes, the brunette "Janet" in the sexy sitcom *Three's Company*—once Joan Jett had come along to make every brunette babe in America use hair gel. The poster has Joyce DeWitt's head photocopied many times. In big bold letters the poster says:

JOYCE DEWITT
JOYCE DEWITT
JOYCE DEWITT

And I think about stealing it, or at least asking for it, but I realize that asking for any of these items is like asking to take home an infectious disease.

Get Your Wings

I AM SITTING IN A BAR staring at a Red Bull ad that references an Aerosmith album that references the film *It's a Wonderful Life*. Every time a bell rings, an angel gets his...and then a shorn lamb with a square head named David asks me if I speak Spanish. I say no. "Not even a little bit?" "Not even a little." "I called you a sexy ghost. Are you here to see the band?" "No. I'm meeting a friend." "Oh, well I don't want to interrupt you meeting a friend." He asks what my name is and extends his hand. "David," he says with his precise rectangular glasses and office shirt. I don't tell him my name. "Why are you not telling me your name?" "Names don't matter to me," I say with a shrug. "Well, it's just polite to tell me," he says. "I go WELL beyond the bounds of politeness most of the time," I say. Now he is asking if I am using my phone to text him or just pretending. "Oh you don't have my number yet!" he calls to me but I ignore him with a smile and finger raised. I guess I am sometimes JUST too polite. Wow, he won't give up! He is fruitlessly mumbling "Jessica... Jessica...JESSica"...asking if he can take me away from my phone for "just ten minutes." He has given up on me for a moment to bond with another stranger and ask if the bartender can turn up the hip-hop. I overhear that he is from San Diego. Now I put down the phone. Oh. He is back. "Can I buy you a drink?" "No." "All right, I'm by myself in here." That is all any of us can expect. "Hey, are you here to see the band?"

Yoni Nanny

ONE OF THE FIRST JOBS I had in Portland was as a nanny for a child who had grown up on a commune. This was a hippie-child with eyes as brown as a muddy creek, ringlets of gold; a child with a face as round as a pumpkin filled with fire on Halloween.

Fire: Her head was hot to the touch as if it contained boiling blood, currents made unstable by growth hormones and inarticulate rage. Her mother looked like a cross between Pocahontas and Liz Taylor. Her father was a ladykilling Pan.

The experiences I have had in my life as a babysitter and nanny showcase to me clearly how I am not equipped to care for any sort of small human life, especially those between the ages of two and four, when hominids can barely speak and constantly leave excretia in their pants, usually as a mode of communication. They cannot express what they want from the adult world by sounds other than wails, moans, and the dull purgatory-throb made by the kicking of feet on a hardwood floor, the chafing of walls with primal fists.

You may think me a child-hater, but I am not. During my nanny experience I tried as hard as I could to romanticize the creature in my care, to feel empathy for her as I would want others to feel empathy for me, if, say, I lost the power of speech and the ability to feed myself.

But the thing was, this hippie-child was a nightmare. Most children I encounter under the age of four seem like alien receptacles of WANT to me—monsters of incalculable ego and exhibitionism—imps sprung from fairy tales capable of masterful feats of manipulation and revenge—yet still so elastic, able to learn in time to control their rage, at least to the cosmetic degree that most adults can.

This was back in the nineties, early in my Portland stay. I took care of this girl for a month, doing her laundry, trying to get her to draw pictures and read books with me. I fed her as best as I could, and held my temper when she shat her pants, which seemed to be an occurrence almost every hour. This child had untapped reservoirs of shit, as if her bowels connected with shit-mines in another dimension, shit which could not—with all of the alchemical prayers of Rocky Mountain commune-dwellers wishing to bring world peace with three dreamcatchers, an old alpaca blanket, a tub of bee pollen and a CD box set of Crosby, Stills and Nash's greatest hits—be turned to gold.

Portland was on the threshold of new development, meaning the demolition of old buildings to make way for "big city" real estate. This town was about to lose its "noir" character as a spiritual home to skinheads, elderly loggers, and retired bikers who claimed to have once been Hell's Angels.

I was a liberal young woman hoping to make the most salient decisions in diet and pocketbook to prevent a future of stark steel boxes in place of old breweries, condos in place of warehouses by the docks that were little more than ivy on crumbling brick. I didn't even LIKE this city, but I wanted to preserve any "beauty that might be lost."

In this conservational spirit, I read a flyer that advertised a town hall meeting where real estate developers would present their plans for "Downtown Revitalization Projects"—one plan which promised to turn a large swath of abandoned industrial blocks into a "European Strolling Village."

There was a snag in my plan. I had to nanny this child for several more hours. In a foolhardy moment of optimism, I decided that I could try to get her in a cheery mood and take her to the meeting.

It was a sunny afternoon in June—hot, sweaty, the last rays of the day casting long shadows off the lumpen oldsters who sat on fire escapes, watering plants and eating unidentifiable boiled things from tins, as operatic as all get-out, like sublime ethereal beings that can travel at the speed of light too long shipwrecked in these bodies, in physical space.

And shipwrecked in a very small body, the antsy soul of a three-year-old begrudgingly took my hand as I tried to walk her several blocks to a hall near the newspaper building where this meeting was going to be.

I remember well the smell of shampoo in this girl's hair, how often it had to be shampooed. I remember how quickly the shade of her face could turn from pale amber to a lurid red. I remember how brown her eyes could look—in a certain light, as dark as black holes.

I remember the stares people would give me as I walked this child along, me in combat boots and cut-off shorts and a body like a sullen teen, as if I was not old enough to care for such a creature... and perhaps I wasn't!

"I yuh...wunnah!" she began to say, her face precipitously close to a cry. Every muscle contorted, raisin-tight. She was ready to pop.

"It will be fun, and there will be cookies," I told her, but every step grew more difficult. Before I knew what was happening she started yelling, in unmistakable English: "Needles in my yoni!"

I knew that hippies commonly used the word "yoni" as a euphemism for vagina, along with "flower" and punani, and womb-loom and honey-hive, but..."Needles in my yoni! They put needles in my yoni!"

I turned as red as this girl was turning. She was bawling.

"Needles in my yoni! They put...needles in my yoni!"

Strangers were turning their heads, strangers in this well-educated white liberal city, many of whom were well acquainted with what the words "needle" and "yoni" meant.

The first thing I could think was, "OH NO! I hope these total strangers don't think that I...put needles in her yoni!"

I started to wonder if this child even knew what these words meant. I wondered if she had learned that saying them made adults feel strange. What on Earth had happened to her?

As I hustled her back up the hill, all I could think of was the high desert mecca of sagebrush and ash and alder and rocks as pink as quartz crystal where this girl grew up in tents and huts with dozens of men with Manson eyes and salt-and-pepper beards and hands that smelled like sunflower seeds and hemp and motor oil, men who may have brandished needles, flesh-needles, with the casual disregard with which they touched fiddles and harmonicas and bongs. I thought of the rage and the shame and the twisted ways of white American men who wished to be shamans and cosmic cowboys and free, like fine thin astral threads the color of sperm hovering high above the Earth's stratosphere, over the moon, each man's anemic spirit an astral albatross.

Later in the night I discussed "needles" with the girl's father. He nodded, his long brown hair in a ponytail, his fringed vest hanging loose about his well-formed arms, his soot-black soul patch, his eyes like those of a plastic doll that can be "put to sleep."

He did not know what to make of her words. He had only recently gotten custody of the girl. Up until this month, he didn't see her more than a couple weeks a year, when he visited the commune. He said the needles were not his own.

Days passed. My life grew silent. My rage diminished when I no longer had to take care of this kid.

In the high desert men become ghost-colored crows. They have beaks like needles, tempers like thorns. In the high desert, men take many forms.

Watch More Reruns

AN OLD WOMAN WITH the body of a decomposing broom and a witch-head of silver cobwebs, she walks across the street in a wind-breaker and a long black skirt and dirty fluorescent sneakers. She has a protest sign in her hand, but from this distance I can't make out what it says. She is chanting something in a high-pitched rasp. She sounds like a death-metal singer and a squalling infant fused together. I realize what I am witnessing is a human crow. I can't tell if she is chanting "March to freedom," or "Watch more reruns," but she is chanting it over and over again and fading into the distance with her tattered cardboard sign.

Lucky Strikes

AT THE BASE OF the white persons' projects a group of women shaped like Hershey's Kisses sit at a picnic table in various states of louche sweatpant disarray smoking menthols and Lucky Strikes. Many of them have half-and-half hair: five inches of gray roots changing abruptly to tips dyed red or a golden-blonde, hauled back in ponytails exposing the architecture of aging faces, all parchment and cliff-face and sun-kissed-but-now-death-gray cheek permanently raised in an infinite series of guffaws. Every one of these women is the color of death. They look like they live in dive bars or in the living rooms they are currently escaping because their high-rise is covered in scaffolding and hammer-BANG-bang-saw. Industrious construction workers in fluorescent orange vests are marching back and forth and hauling things and moving with the bionic speed of stupid superheroes. Yes, I think superheroes are stupid, and I will NOT stand corrected!

One of the women sees me and says, "Hey ther's some amazing eyes you got there, GURL," and I thank her and think of her enormous muscular calves and her untucked flannel shirt over cut-off shorts, and decide she is the healthiest of the gang.

The other women...oh God, they are dying of diabetes, like the one with little clumps of matted hair in the wheelchair, she is all flesh and balding head, and there is the one who looks like an old French theorist who has been transported to the outskirts of Milwaukie, with that Asiatic quality to the eyes French women get when they are really old, and she looks like she is made of a wig and two capsules and a pint of bourbon and hand lotion mixed together like an alchemical recipe for all-seeing-eye-witch. And the Hispanic lady who looks like she was once the most beautiful woman in the galaxy but now she is deflated, and also gray, and holding onto that cigarette for dear life in her bulging high-waisted jeans. The flesh struggles to stay in one place on that pouty-lipped sexpot skull but her organs, her feet, her every body part are deserting...along with the mind, but that one lone greaser guy next to her, he is still trying to get some.

And these ladies, despite looking like they no longer want to be alive, they are more alive than almost everyone as they suck in their smoke and feel the breeze on their faces, and their words come out like the groans of baby cougars you overhear in nature documentaries. They snort and cough and comment and they are truly in the now because there is no other place for their molecules to be going to, not ever.

Joe Camel

ONCE I FOUND A COLLECTION of Joe Camel T-shirts in a free box next to a dumpster downtown. This was next to my apartment building, and I speculated upon which resident might have worn all of these Joe Camel T-shirts. My first guess was that it might be the old man down the hall who wore a gas station attendant's jacket every single day, even though he appeared to have no job to go to. I would bet you anything his name was Roy or Red or Earl. He had ancient emerald eyes in a face that had grown to resemble an orange rind, a nose so deformed by alcohol, it would give Karl Malden a run for his money. He wore his hair in what I would have to call a "reduced" pompadour, because there wasn't much hair left to fashion into a pompadour; yet fashion he did, and in the fluorescent hall light, in passing, one could even count the tooth-marks left by the comb in his emaciated coif. He always reeked of smoke. His apartment only had a cot and a spare card table. I bet if I saw him now I would even think him sexy, but at the time I was just a kid, a practical joker. Pipe cleaner men held no power o'er my raging libido. I was such a practical joker that I decided to use these twenty Joe Camel T-shirts in some sort of epic performance art piece. They reeked heavily of smoke. I never bothered to wash them. I kept them stuffed in a paper grocery bag in the back of my closet for two years, until I realized I would NEVER make a work of art with them, and I put them back on the streets where they belonged.

Skull

AT 11:42 ON A SUNDAY NIGHT the bus from Clackamas has run twenty minutes late and when it finally does arrive on the strip of highway where I stand like a high-class escort in a black fur coat, I get on and seat myself next to a man who is dressed like a rap star and he nervously keeps looking back, to the back of the bus, at someone or something, and the bus is packed like a can of Pringles and I expect that this man with his darting head is actually a mad shooter and any minute he's gonna rise from his seat with an accomplice or two and riddle the lot of us with holes leaking bile-black blood in slow motion under the strobing fluorescent lights above our heads that make skin and eyeballs and thoughts a gray-green hue. We are tinted like tin; color us hungry.

The bus is packed. Where are all of us rushing at this hour? To get downtown, to get to the bars overflowing on Labor Day? It feels like a party-bus full of women with emery-board skin and light dustings of freckles over sweatpants, ponytails, long hours as nurses, caregivers, strippers, gluing furniture together with foul epoxy in factories which no one understands. These sweatpant women lazily press buttons on phones, and smile as if they are on their way to meet boyfriends, or controversially affectionate Dobermans, or vodka tonics. Their secret smiles tell me that even though the night is old, their hearts are young and they need release before sleep.

Two men in shabby clothes from somewhere in Africa speak with thick accents which make all of the zombie-Americans turn their heads in curiosity and fear; so long as no one does anything sudden, or funny, things will be okay, say the sideways glances. The men from Africa are old, and their skin hangs on their faces like an art installation, like flesh made from pancake batter: Pancake eyes, pancake cheeks, and ears, shoes tied and toes tapping, in wait for whatever is downtown, downtown.

A man with a sea-captain-red face and a sea-captain-white beard compulsively takes notes in a spiral-bound notebook. I sense that he was once some kind of artist, or botanist, or activist, or architect, or wannabe politico. He is a West Coast archetype who may have once run with the wolves, or Ken Kesey. He is dislodged in time; even the way his raincoat hangs on his shoulders tells me that he doesn't know why he is alive anymore, transported, as if by a science-fiction device, to this strange year named Two-Thousand-Fifteen.

Numerous young men with office haircuts who look like they just got off work from shoe stores and call centers are also on the bus, their hormones directing them to my eyes and my legs. I watch them watching me, but what I am really watching is the SKULL.

For the longest time I thought it was a real old lady, but the way her large gray sneaker was tapping, so quickly; the way the very musculature of her face was straining to suck her lips in and out of her mouth, like a human crossed with a guppy; the way her nose was crushed, collapsed, little more than an indentation in her skull, and the way the skin of her forehead, while there were sores...the skin itself had no wrinkles. Her eyes, though sunken, had a moisture, a firmness that was disconcerting. Her body was so shrunken...but there was something off! She was shaped like an old lady, her face had collapsed like an old lady, but in her motions...oh, my!

She wore crimson corduroy pants and a dirty gray puffer jacket. A green ski hat was on her head, and her skull was so deprived of fat that the hat nearly eclipsed her ears and cheekbones altogether—but the wisps of hair poking out, they were of a rich brown color. This was not old-lady hair, despite most of it seeming to have been yanked out, merging with scabs that she scraped at with her...well-manicured and YOUNG hands!

Yes, it was the hands, in the end, that gave it away. I have more white roots and older-looking hands than this creature! This woman was probably thirty, thirty-five! Maybe even a very tweaked-out twenty-eight, but she had done a real number on her body, irreversible damage; inordinate amounts of crystals snorted up that collapsed, battered shape on her face—a siphon which was once a nose, on a face that may have once been beautiful.

It is usually the beauties who turn out this way—lookers at twelve, and corpses by thirty. After I watched her twitch and swivel, she got up to lean on a pole with such a seductive posture that I could easily imagine the woman she once was.

Had she any idea of what she had become? Did she look in the mirror and see a healthy face superimposed over this barely-breathing skull? At first glance, she looked eighty, I mean, seriously, eighty without a nose—and then—those hands, and other, subliminal details alert me to the secret of her youth!

I imagined what would happen if I was a tweaker on this astronomical scale. I imagine getting to such a psychedelic high, such an unearthly, holy sensation of cracking open my skull, being superhuman...and getting addicted to it, to the point that even when my looks fade, my everything else fades, I think to myself, "So what? That's the price I pay for enlightenment, for superpowers!" What else CAN you think in such a state?

What was this bird-lady-Harry-Dean-Stanton made of broom handles, oily rags, psychic stains...what was she bopping off to find this fine evening downtown-way?

Velvet Armor

WHEN I WAS A YOUNGSTER in Portland I met a famous older writer, the one who was straight rather than the one who was gay. It was a small town, so there were not very many famous older writers to go around. He was caustic, rarely smiled. He was already going gray and had a fashion sense I'd call soccer dad meets Panamanian drug lord. He always wrote about sex. It was faceless and sharp and thwarted. You felt transaction and neglect jabbing with every description, like a styrofoam carton of turkey broken open in a paper grocery bag.

At one point I had him on my radio show. After that he had my number and he'd call me once in a while. While I had given him some of my stories to read, he never mentioned them, and I had no illusions about him thinking of me as a peer. I was just a woman with a pretty face who could stand his sense of humor.

The time came when he, being of "a certain age," was told by his doctor to get his prostate checked. The doc gave him some sort of exploratory scrape or biopsy, or whatever it is they do to prostates. (I'm as clueless about proctology as men are about what gynecologists do when they get their thumbs juiced-up to the cervix.)

So the writer called me up in distress, because after the docs did this thing, whatever it was, his prostrate was swollen and hurt. It didn't feel bad at ALL before—but now it was a terrible mess and he couldn't help but sit on it every day and worry.

A couple weeks later my writer-friend called again. He was in a severe funk. The swelling had gotten worse. The docs checked out his prostate and said that there was now scar tissue and an infection from whatever they'd done. He had to take pain medication and antibiotics. He was supposed to restrict his diet. His sex drive was entirely gone—the minute this prostate business blew up, he didn't feel comfortable finding any woman to relent to his jabbing ways. He was, after several decades of feeling like a young punk, having a midlife crisis.

It was when he went on for forty minutes about his prostate that I decided not to encourage him further. My life was mixed up as it was.

But the thing is, I am now much older than I was then. I am starting to think about whether romantic partners would still love me if some part of my body stopped working, or was REMOVED!

You know women do have to, on occasion, get their breasts and uterus (uteri?) removed. It happens far more than we want to think about, although Breast Cancer Awareness Pumpkins, Reproductive Heath Consciousness Loaves of Bread, and Refillable Hysterectomy Education Juice Bottles attempt to remind us all the time of the battlefield that comes with aging and prolonged exposure to toxins, like the air we breathe.

I wonder what I would feel if I found out that I had to have my uterus removed. My mother did. My grandmother had hers yanked out in her early thirties, because it was not working for her at the time. Most of the women I've met who have had hysterectomies speak of being relieved, as if the uterus, with its lumps and cramps and pains, was some sort of ball and chain that never did them any good! These women have become lean and masculine and no-nonsense with their youthful hormones out of the way. They act with less timidity. They act like they are here to get things DONE, and no one is going to stop them.

I'm not saying this as an ad for hysterectomies, here. I mean, my mother had one and acts like the same whimsical shut-in she was pre-hysterectomy, so this magical process I'm describing does not happen with every uterus-free woman.

I am just thinking about love, and how much of a person's body can be removed with one's lover still feeling he or she is interacting with a "whole" human being.

What if I had all of my sex organs removed? What if I didn't even HAVE a vagina anymore? Would it be fair for me to expect anyone to have a romantic relationship with me then? Here, try this armpit instead! I'll squeeze it real tight and it will do the job!

Well, of course it depends on how shallow one's lover is. It also depends on what stage of life one's lover is in. I wouldn't expect an eighteen-year-old to be able to handle a relationship with a woman who had no breasts or vagina, as terrible as this sounds! (Or vice versa, switch the sexes any way you please, folks.) When you're young, you should live it up, if you can.

Love is a complicated matter. No one ever loves once, and rarely does anyone sustain passion forever—yet we are such irrational creatures in love. We want it ALL, and we want it FOREVER.

Say I had fallen in love with prostate man. I was a kid, twenty-eight at the time. Would I accept what he was at sixty, a fogey obsessed with his health, or would I be yearning for something he ONCE was, when he was a punk of twenty-eight? Would I pore over photos of him once-smiling, once "free"—whatever free means, and yearn for a type of adventure he claimed he was no longer capable of having?

Age—and love. I think about these things as I move away from youth and into a new territory. My spirit remains as defiant as ever, but I see that as I age, my body starts to do strange things. All of our bodies are starting to do strange things. Our minds are DOING EVEN STRANGER things! Death creeps closer, but maturity is the salve. I wouldn't trade the life I have at my current age for any spirit-jizz that powered me at eighteen.

But do you wonder...what happens in there, beneath the velvet armor of skin? Do you wonder where these bodies will lead us?

Bungeedollcase

IT IS NINETEEN DEGREES. Plump flakes of dry white are gathering on the ground like the contents of a broken pillow, and in this searing haze I have SIGHTED THIS SPECIMEN. See him now: A macho dude in bungee-stuntwear of cut-off khaki shorts, those brown hiking sneakers that look like they're made out of dreadlocks and nylon rope. He is making his way down the street. His calves are enormous, as if they contain reservoirs of liquid plutonium. Wind slices at his face. Underneath his stubble, his cheeks are red as a baboon's ass. He walks with a goony stride, clutching a pale pink little girl's doll case as if he is going to an important meeting.

The Living Entombed and My Lemon-Fresh Pledge

WHEN I WAS TWELVE YEARS OLD, I was in Catholic school, and we were supposed to be doing "training" for our Confirmation—for the non-Catholics amongst you (and trust me, I was harboring atheistic feelings back then, so don't feel you're offending me by THAT) I will fill you in on what Confirmation is: You are supposed to do good deeds or "responsible acts" that demonstrate that you have graduated from being a child to an adult in the eyes of your community. Now you are still supposed to abstain from sex and never have an abortion if you do, but you are an "adult" anyway!

One of the many tasks we had to do was clean the homes of elderly people who could no longer care for themselves. These were elderly people who had not been sent to old folks' homes, but they were discovered to be incapacitated in ways that their own children (if they had any) did not want to deal with.

In one of these homes, there was an old lady who lived in piles of garbage. She was very frail, very emaciated, perhaps in her nineties: Everything about her, her skin, her hair, the look in her eyes—had gone white, puckered, grown inward, grown nowhere. A lot of these old folks seemed to inhabit a mental twilight as dim as the rooms in which they lived—rooms that may once have been fresh with the air from open windows, free of clutter, clean and as full of potential as a furniture display in a department store.

If you looked on the walls of these old people, you'd see photographs of these very same rooms, yet back in time—thirty or forty years earlier, when these humans still had light in their eyes.

I saw this happen with my own grandparents. Their moldy little house in Syracuse (yes, I grew up with them in a sublime megalopolis of mold) grew more cluttered as they approached death. The piles of junk, meaning old newspapers, pyramids of unattended plastic bags, broken furniture and objects that could just not be moved anymore, grew so great that to take a photograph, my mother had to (and she still does this, to this DAY) spend ten minutes moving the piles to another area of the room so that the picture would appear to be taken in a "normal" house. There IS NO NORMAL.

But back to the houses of old people that were on the docket for cleaning: You would find the most bizarre extensions of each person's mental state left on end-tables, or near the doors they exited less and less frequently.

After a certain age, the disorder of your house (and the intimacy of your house) reflects the disorder of your brain. Next to an old lady's door you might find several broken tubes of lipstick, REAMS of discarded Kleenex, and those wax crayons that old folks use to cover their white roots between sporadic dye jobs. You might find hairspray on a windowsill, or whiskey bottles piled at the foot of an old man's bed. Why get up? Except to obtain more whiskey. Every house felt like a seething, pulsing extension of its occupant's brain.

We were just kids trying to deal with this garbage! There had to be an "after" that looked better than the "before." We didn't always know what to do other than wipe the counters and clean the toilets, and try to throw away anything that was empty or broken.

In one bathroom of this particularly old lady, there was a lot of dirt. In fact the entire house smelled like rotting squirrels and the three of us (we were three girls in our little plaid skirts and knee socks) had to remain in this house for hours, unable to leave or cease shuffling, under penalty of nuns. There was no way to crack a window, because there was too much junk to get to the windows.

I ended up with bathroom duty. The stench was particularly strong in there. For all I knew, the woman may have had twenty dead kittens rotting under a stack of thirty-year-old *Prevention* magazines. I have since read many stories about cases such as this.

As I cleaned that bathroom, I had one unexpected reprieve—a bottle of lemon spray-disinfectant that I used liberally, because as I sprayed the fuck out of that bathroom, the cancer-causing synthetic lemon chemicals in this bottle (that was dwindling fast) were relieving me of the scent of dying animal.

I thought of how ironic this would appear to my classmates. At the time, I was going through my non-bathing period. There was a day where I went to bed without taking off my uniform, and this felt so simple, so easy, that I just kept wearing it all week without bathing. These weeks turned into months. Then it became an entire year, between the ages of twelve and thirteen, where I ceased to bathe at all. I only washed my hands and face because, despite smelling like a bum, I needed to have fresh makeup every twelve hours or so.

I use this as evidence that I was NOT a dirt lightweight: This woman had DEAD THINGS in her house, which we did not find or try to find.

I say all of this because I am thinking about houses and their occupants. I can generally tell, as I'm walking past a house, the age group of those who live inside—just based on their color schemes, the sorts of cars in their driveways, and the plants on their porches. Curtains and landscaping reveal quite a lot! And oh, those lone houses with venetian blinds, through which you see snow-white tufts of hair poking, as an elderly Irish man reads a newspaper in a room as sterile as a dentist's office. Those rooms...those waiting rooms for death!

Last week I walked by a house where a very stained mattress was left out front. It looked like it was stained a pale brown by either urine or blood, and a lot of it was focused on one side, as if someone had died and just MELTED into the fabric of the mattress top.

I looked at the house and had confirmation: Yep. Old folks' house. DEFINITE old folks' house.

And I thought of our culture and how we ARE, here in America, the most isolated from death of all the peoples on this planet, mainly because isolation from death is BIG MONEY.

Yes, big money: Every hospital, mortuary, and food-n-fun-advertiser on the planet has found a way to make death look like something that ALWAYS HAPPENS TO OTHER PEOPLE, but only on TINY SCREENS and BIG, SURROUND-SOUND screens.

By isolating death to a spectacle that we never really get to taste but always fear is around the corner, DEATH HAS BEEN TURNED INTO PORNOGRAPHY that we must pay for, in a rainbow of media peep-shows. This cannot be sustained.

If you ever want to do something with a loved one's dead body that is "different" than the standard interment and cremation (like attach fifty lbs of TNT to the deceased while surrounding him with the positive vibes of a peyote-fueled orgy) you have to go through LEGAL PROCEDURES to claim the blood of your blood, the loves of your life. Now do you start to think about how our isolation from death is a big business, with lobbyists and everything?

Houses...isolation, and the intimacy of an old woman's mess. And that is all.

Krishna-Krishna

WHEN I LIVED IN LONDON, I became obsessed with cooking. I was obsessed with cooking because I was anorexic. I was anorexic because I had given birth to a child and had just given her up for adoption. I was all of nineteen. I had no time to be anorexic or be a cook as I was building props for a theatre and staying out late hanging out with an old man named Gerald who always wore a trench coat and read tarot cards in hotel lobbies. I think he was homeless. As I have realized recently, most of the people I hung out with in London were old enough to be my grandparents. I can't tell you why things happened this way, but I would wander around and look in people's eyes, and I didn't connect with a lot of young folks.

I would wander through markets and late-night cafés, and take notes, compulsively, and when I got hungry, I would go to the Hare Krishna temple and eat Indian food. Nothing comes for free, of course: The longer you eat free food (I went there at least three times a week) prepared by religious folk, the stronger grow their demands that you pay attention to the platitudes, attitudes, myth-whiffs that come with the meal.

And so I slowly but surely heard the life stories of each and every thirty-something Krishna-monk, mostly ex-skinheads, punks, burnouts, addicts, and kids who came from abusive homes. They would bashfully eat their desserts, the sweetened-burned milk balls that in texture and size were exactly like honey-flavored testicles, and while chewing these milk balls, slowly, tenderly, they would tell me their stories of being raped or hurt or hurting others in a million ways.

These guys, beneath their imported Indian scarves and ill-fitting slippers, they had been SO BROKEN that they needed a religion to erase their memories, literally wipe the slate clean. I thought of their conversion this way: Identity bankruptcy. Religion as suicide.

One of the last times I ate with the boys, I ended up going to their ceremony afterwards. Indian families (not lily-whites at all) filled a room with sleepy eyes and toddlers in tow, and from what I recall, there was chanting and a lot of swaying back and forth to a tambourine as if we were all on roofies. It was mind-numbingly dull for me, despite the details I drank in. I knew I had reached the end of the free meal ticket, coz I would now be expected to go to these foot-drag-a-thons every other day to earn my keep.

As I left the temple, I thought of one of the most amusing Hare Krishna beliefs: that whatever you are thinking about at the moment of your death will directly influence the body you reincarnate into. In other words, if you die with "base desires," or demeaning imagery on your mind, you will likely be reborn as an armadillo, or maybe an earthworm. On the other hand, if you die while chanting the name of your god, you may break the incarnation cycle altogether, and ascend to some misty sluice of heavenly bliss, like a breadbasket in an amber-scented ether that stretches on for eternity.

I was laughing to myself when leaving the temple for the last time, already missing the sad monks with their shattered eyes and scarred foreheads. I was thinking this: What if there was a man who died while watching a fly clamber on the back of a turd. He would be wheezing his last breath and watching the fly's iridescent body glistening in the afternoon sun. And this dying man watching the fly...would he spend his next life as a fly, or as a startlingly self-conscious turd?

Gary the Swinger

GARY THE SWINGER IS OBSESSED with longevity. He holds up his phone and shows off the men he has had sex with as if he is pointing out appetizers on a menu. So many appetizers—but which ones are a main course? There is no main course. Gary is like a sex anorexic. He binges and purges, but it is essential that he never gain weight, feel full. He has a sauna in his basement. Once he had a lodger in his basement, too, a meth-head who paid rent. One day the lodger snuck into Gary's car and stabbed him in the neck. The knife went through the headrest of Gary's seat and into one of his main arteries. Gary was afraid of peeling himself out of his seat, for fear that he would start to lose blood. With the knife pinning him to his seat, he drove to an emergency room and honked his horn until the medics could remove him from his seat in a way that wouldn't kill him. This is the story Gary tells. I presume that the tweaker jumped out of the car and didn't ride to the hospital in Gary's back seat. Gary forgave his meth-head-lodger-assailant. The dude was probably cute and had a big dick. Wonders never cease.

Slurpee Cum-Shot

WHEN I WAS EIGHTEEN YEARS OLD I dated a late-night K-mart janitor. We were the only ones in the store one night, which was simultaneously a sociological dream come true and incredibly mundane. In the break room there was a small black-and-white tee-vee and Orwellian signs posted every three steps about the importance of employee loyalty. While my boyfriend, a wiry ska-listening cherub with an Afro as big as the moon danced across the floors with a Zamboni, I decided to make myself a complimentary Slurpee. In my delirium—possibly a drunken delirium—the enormous paper cup of Slurpee-ice slipped out of my hands and fell to the floor, where the cup remained, while the contents of the cup ricocheted off of the ground, flying five feet in the air, and hitting my face. I rapidly tried to wipe the vivid red Slurpee-juice out of my eyes, off of my cheeks, running to the bathroom, laughing hysterically, and then with alarm: Try as I might, the Slurpee fluid, made of corn syrup and red number five-thousand, had, upon ten seconds of contact with my nose, forehead, and cheeks, dyed my flesh. I spent fifteen minutes trying to soap it off, and consequently never drank a Slurpee again.

Dead Friends, Dead Relationships, and a Dead Hairbrush

A LONG TIME AGO I lived in an apartment building filled with street urchin youths and old men hacking up lungs on an hourly basis. The building was constantly filled with the biologically vivid noises of sex and death.

Whenever one of the old ones would die, their less consequential belongings would be laid out in the mail room, in the hopes that these Skoal-stained pillows, ceramic kittens, and half-cracked Mason jars could be given new life.

In such a way I inherited a dead man's spices, and slowly but surely used them in my cooking. Not being superstitious, I didn't feel I would be harmed by these crumpled baggies of oregano and dollar-bin tubes of celery seeds; however, my imagination did run wild. At moments I would visualize a cold vein of anti-life creeping from a baggie of oregano to my hands and then, say, to a nutritional yeast sauce, or a pan of sautéed eggplant.

I also have a dead man's tea. Fifteen years ago I was at a garage sale and purchased a Vietnam vet's tea collection. He had tea tins from all over the Far East with elaborate mythological murals on their sides. These teas were harvested and sealed in plastic pouches and pushed inside these rainbow-colored tins before Thailand and Taiwan had telephone poles, before China was anything other than a nation of Mao's children, pod-people limping along in abject poverty, several gaps in each family for fathers, babies, wives, where the murderous years of the Cultural Revolution were freshly felt. The vet's tins were from the late seventies. They were already old when I purchased them at his garage sale. He presided over his pile with a dark and manic fury, placing my money in a metal box while expressing to me that caffeine was made by the devil and that anyone who drinks it will suffer a premature death. He was not making a light comical observation; he meant this stuff.

I honestly can't imagine this man is alive today. I feel justified in calling his tea "Dead Man's Tea."

I still have his tea. His stockpile was large. When I am out of my preferred teas, I meter out the vet's tea, and in this way I time-travel, I observe the memory of the world in which it was produced.

Today I use a dead woman's hairbrush. She was a friend who was often drunk or on pills or recovering from another suicide attempt. As she did with her bloodstream, she also binged and purged with her belongings.

She had more wealth than she knew what to do with. She had a job working for the engineering department of the Bonneville Dam. Her ability to make elaborate calculations kept her in Chanel, in Prada, in furs, and later on in Dilaudid, in Stoli, in Maker's Mark.

Her father died of cancer and she spent a year collecting addictions, taking so much work leave that her employers retired her at age thirty-four, with a pension that would maintain her in the fashion she was accustomed to living.

My friend had a death wish and way too much time on her hands. She missed her father. She wanted to join him. She flew to tropical islands, to jungles, to Miami. She kept the company of men—new ones every night, the more manly the better.

She was attracted to the strutters, the ones with mustaches and angry mouths. They played rap songs ten years out of date, drove tuned-up muscle cars, had collections of stolen guitars.

After waking from blackouts she would discover these men in her bed, this money missing. When there weren't men, there were piles of new purchases flooding her closets and threatening to bury her in a way that no amount of oxycodone could do.

Once she took me to a hookah bar. She fluttered like a nervous butterfly around an Israeli man; he was all shaven head, muscle, a carob stallion in freshly laundered Hurley cargo shorts and canvas shoes. She draped her body and mine in sequined scarves that were meant to make us genies, turn our white bodies brown, make us desirable to men like the stallion.

Through smoke and neon light I watched the stallion shuffle, evade. He was embarrassed to show his friends that he had interest in this girl. Later she took him to a suite of her apartment decorated in bamboo and a hundred colored veils. She said that in private he treated her rough, and she liked it this way.

During one of her purges, I was called by a mutual friend: He said I'd better show up at her place because she was getting rid of things that I could sell on Ebay. Time was of the essence, he stressed. I felt like I was in a real-life game show.

My boyfriend agreed to drive me to her apartment. On the way there, he shook his head and lectured me. He said I was a person of dubious morals taking advantage of a woman in distress.

I said, "She's going to throw her hoard away, whether I come to look through it or not!"

In his duct-taped sports car, the man drove me to my friend's luxury rooms, her carpets wet with beer, two snow-white impulse-buy kittens lurking in the corners and staring at us like Keane children.

She whooped with joy when we arrived, and then she shed tears as, clearly under the influence of substances, she mentioned she was recovering from an overdose that almost killed her. She asked me to go through her two closets, and take whatever she had left in them.

There wasn't as much to take as you would think. She had already put her favored items in storage, and what remained was either too damaged or too out-of-style to sell. Once I was done sorting through her goods, she pleaded with us to sit down so that she could tell us stories.

Two weeks before this visit she had been driven to a hospital, dead on arrival. Several attempts were made to revive her. On the last try, as an assistant was filling out her death certificate, her pulse returned.

She spoke of how eerie it was to still be alive. She told us how she felt that while she was "out of her body," she had contacted her dead father. She didn't understand why she had to "be back."

Then she showed us a box of medallions, which she won running marathons. This was a shoebox filled with thirty or forty medallions. They were made of a heavy silver. They made substantial noises as she ran her manicured fingers through the gleaming heap. She was listless, clearly on opiates, yet craving a drink and offering us beer.

She showed us jewelry made by an internet friend whom she called her fiancé. In two jewelry boxes, bronze-plated insects made out of watch parts sat like alien food, like abandoned limbs, like the gifts of a man who lives far away and has no intention of visiting.

"There's a word for this sort of thing...they are steampunk, aren't they? Aren't they pretty? My fiancé made them. If I wasn't engaged to be married, I'd be all over you," she said to my boyfriend. She squeezed his arms, admired his broad shoulders, his lion's mane.

"You are a lot of man, oh you are! You are lucky, Jen!" she told me.

I thought, *oh, if you only knew...*

Then she asked us to go to a bar with her. We did. It was a dive bar, and the men inside wore ski caps, faded black. People were here to get wasted, not to feel chic.

As we drank, we heard stories of my friend's family. She came from prosperity, both financial and physical. Her family was vast, with brothers, sisters, aunts, a whole lot of people who talked to each other and had festivals celebrating the fecundity of their stock. I and my boyfriend, having both been raised in small families who were distrustful of society and frugal to a point of paranoia—found her descriptions of the resorts she spent her childhood in to be exotic, like fairy tales.

Despite the bounty of her youth, despite the personalities of loved ones she vividly described, my friend could not hold on to firm ground.

As we were leaving the bar and about to drive her back to her apartment, she pointed to my hair, which was dyed black. She told me that despite my hair and dark eyeliner, I was only dark on the outside, and that no one would ever be as dark on the inside as she was.

I didn't believe this, but I wasn't going to argue, either. The man who raised her had died a year before, and she wasn't able to recover. Within a year, she was dead.

My boyfriend and I went to the wake, a large affair where several families converged—her biological family, her "party" family, and members of her AA group. The wake was in a banquet room of a Unitarian church—clean, with large windows that let in a milky light, a carpet that reminded me of grade school. There were silver platters of food, pitchers of herbal tea. I listened as people from both the "successful" and the "lost" parts of my friend's life spoke about her "infectious smile," her need to "fully live."

I wondered what the "country" relations thought of her "city" relations—the drag queens, the bad boys, the artists of strange volume, scrambled mind. I wondered if the Israeli stallion knew she was dead, or if she was a distant memory to him, like a cologne he had worn for a week and discarded.

Toward the end of the wake, there was a slide show. Images of my friend as a small child drifted across a screen, as the songs of Billy Joel crooned and slithered like a silver gel. I felt tears, hot and unfamiliar, stream down my face.

In a matter of seconds, I felt complicated emotions of sadness and revenge rise in my craw. Aha! My waterworks for a woman I barely knew would not stop, and the boyfriend who thought I was ruthless to take clothes she was throwing away would see...once and for all...that my heart was a muscle...of mush!

Weeks passed. The hairbrush I was using fell apart. All of the spokes fell out. I started using my boyfriend's hairbrush. In a fit of anger, he threw it on the ground, and it broke in two.

We never saved the money to buy a new hairbrush. Replacing a hairbrush seemed like an afterthought. I tried, in a creative gesture, to repair our shared hairbrush. I covered it in packing tape and a huge silver bow.

Moments came when he became upset at me. He told me I was betraying him, stealing from him in ways I did not understand.

He would chase me, and scream, and punch the walls, and I would feel strange about using the repaired brush with its silver bow. It became a reminder of a cycle I had to escape. I needed to no longer live with this man—and I needed a new hairbrush.

I remembered that in the bags I had taken from my troubled friend's apartment, one of her hairbrushes had made its way into the piles of junk. Late one night, I searched and searched...and found it. It was dirty, covered in the fallen-out debris of hair extensions. My friend was very interested in having hair extensions, but the dark side of extensions is that they shed a glue-like substance that coats the brush of one who attempts to groom them. I tried my best to clean out the debris, and this became my "private" brush.

Being in a possessive relationship makes a woman strive to make almost everything she touches "private." You try to escape the eyes, the questions. You want to escape the names. It doesn't matter what you *actually* are! Your world becomes a never-ending quest for privacy.

I live in the shadow of a relationship I had with a man who is now dead to me.

I still use my dead friend's hairbrush. I just washed my hair, and I decided that I would try to get more of her extension-glue out of the spokes.

In life, my friend was too intense to be around for long. Her pain was so great, and her need to buy friends with oblivion was also great. If she bought you drinks, she was trying to buy time away from a pain that snaked through her head, a pain that always lay in wait.

Despite her abilities in science, she could not move past death. She chose death to end loss. Loss could not be comprehended in any rational way.

Long Distance

I WAS THREE THOUSAND MILES from the park, the night, the over-lords of the underworld where the shooting took place. I was as far as one could get from the Portland double-whammy of greased poles and meth-mouth: I was in the pipe-heat and lamplight of my mother's house—my mother, a good Catholic girl turned sixty-eight, who hadn't felt the caress of a man or a sip of alcohol in forty years.

I was in the throes of my yearly visit to her—a visit that would inevitably take me back in time as well as space. My mother appeared to absorb information about the year 2013 through the sealed glass walls of a time capsule. To visit her, as I did for two weeks every year, was to submit to her rules—some spoken, some unspoken:

The tee-vee was omnipresent. I was not to leave the house unless she served as my escort. I was not to walk on the grass due to the peril of avian flu, poison rabbit pellets, flesh-eating ticks transmitted by herds of mutant deer. And then there were the people—rapists behind every storefront, in parking lots, even in banks. The dangers of the outside world were limitless.

After two or three hours of a visit I would feel decades of my adult life peel away and my skin grow raw and submissive under my mother's care—my soul inert within its wrapper, like a slab of overtenderized beef. I would lose the will to fight. If I proposed the idea of my leaving the house, solo, she would respond with panic; too many words. It was better to yield, to hide.

I didn't have a computer. My cell phone bill wasn't paid. I only had my mother's landline with the number I memorized as a small child, and here I was, at age thirty-nine, getting the call that this woman I didn't know very well—this woman who was the party girl, the troubled blonde, the pill-head was found dead, a gunshot wound to the head. It was reported as a homicide.

My boyfriend was on the phone. He acted so delicate when he told me. It was as if he was easing into the story with fiber-optic fore-play, semantic lube, a type of sentimentality that people use when they finally get a chance to say some really juicy bad news, and for once in their lives, the messenger can sound virtuous by getting the words right.

Her body was found in a park outside of the city—past the thirty or so blocks called "Felony Flats"—past trailer parks, condo row-houses, past Max tracks and ranch homes listing in sinkholes—past *more* clumps of trailers and endless strip clubs, endless like a mermaid's necklace made of pearls, each miniature orb discolored, a glaucous eye.

Her body was found with a gunshot to the head, having cooled for several hours on an October night—a clear night before the rainy season—Indian Summer, they say. Within twenty-four hours, three people were taken in as suspects for murder, including a woman who, the prosecution says, was fascinated with death: working as a mortuary assistant, owning guns and posing in pictures with them—one gun called Bonnie, another named Clyde. Clyde was the killer.

My boyfriend repeated what the news told him: Video surveillance showed our blonde meeting the killers outside of a strip club. They may have been meeting under the pretense of selling her drugs, or more likely, hearing that she had a lot of money and she wanted to buy them *all* drugs, stay out all night long.

I remember well that this is how she operated once she had a few drinks in her. She offered to pay for anyone around her: buy gifts, manicures, meals, keep the party going until dawn, mid-afternoon, maybe forever.

In such a state, she could be happy. She could grope, kiss, or cry for death.

My boyfriend told me this, the tidbit in the news that seemed the most implausible, and I got a chill:

It is common for suspects, upon being apprehended—if they do not have the best legal counsel—to spout wild alibis, excuses, fantasy stories that absolve them of personal guilt. The one item that could be used to show that the killers were "not in their right minds" was actually the detail that made the most sense to me...

Two of the suspects were a couple about to get married. The night of the murder was supposed to be an early start to their honeymoon.

The three defendants were doing the rounds of strip clubs before meeting my friend. They said the victim got into their Cadillac and rode around with them until they got to a park, where they were going to do some "target practice." The wedding couple had sex while my friend spoke to the third suspect. My friend was getting "louder" as the minutes passed. The three say that she became hysterical and was asking them to kill her. To finally shut her up, one of them shot her, and the others congratulated him. Then the three drove away in a coal-black Cadillac—a car as black as death and the night sky— alien stars winking without soul, without fanfare in outer space.

Images of Jim Morrison singing "Break on Through to the Other Side" and every cliché of death as "liberation" rather than a gloomy walk with sinners through an endless vale, filled my mind.

The other side...my friend thirsted for it. Would she do anything to get it, including asking these shaky, black-hole strangers hopped up on bullets and forever?

𝓝𝑒𝓌 𝓐𝑚𝑒𝓇𝒾𝒸𝑎𝓷

THERE IS A MAN WHO is new to America and he doesn't know whether it is right or wrong to be chivalrous, because sex is so confusing. Women with shaved heads call each other dude, but kiss men, and smoke doobies in public, and wait for the New American to get on the bus first because he was at the bus stop first. He feebly waves his arm to let the ladies go, but they hang back, and he resigns himself to step on before them. His brown skin confuses people. He gets up and offers ladies in dresses his seat, but they don't take it. He offers his personal space less and less frequently. He no longer tries to smile, or nod, or ask if people like the sunshine. He buries his face in a paperback book, even though he has a phone. He is slowly but surely becoming an American.

Going for baroque

The season of the witch happened
to be a crisp day in April

As a child I manufactured friends

A survivor of the social experiment
we call the Twentieth Century

These seats are taken

Party of one

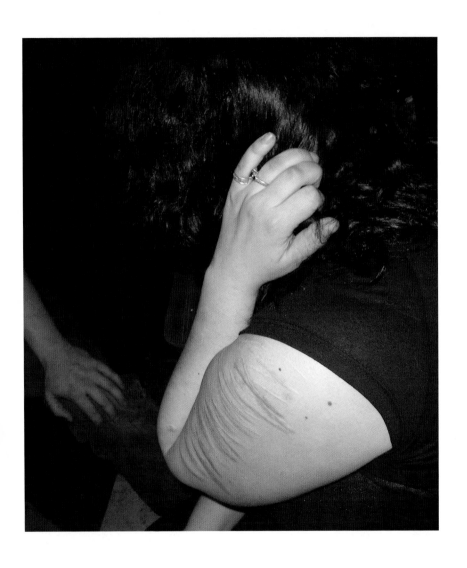

How deep can you go,
without going too deep?

Dime-store diatribes

The Life Penalty

No finer poetry can you find

Fighting for the virtues of meat thermometers and beautiful hair

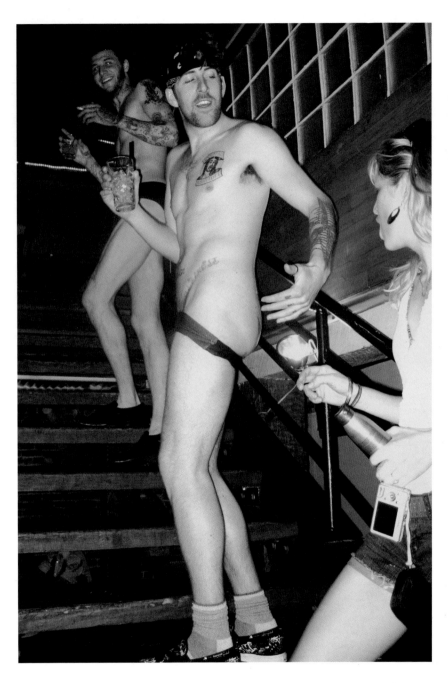

Does this life make my ass look fat?

Their wallets are full of leaves

STOCK TIPS FROM MARS

Performing at The Hour That Stretches

A sourpuss in Olympus

Mother Call Gynecologist

I SPEAK TO MY MOTHER on the phone once a week. When doing this I commit to an act of traveling through time as well as space. Specifically, I am traveling to Syracuse, New York, to the year Nine-teen-Fifty-Eighty-Seventy-Four-Sixty-ish-Forty-Nine-Seventy-Two. My mother never left these years. Her body, a loose configuration of atoms in a blood-sack, continues to pace back and forth over one patch of land, as the Earth hurls ever forward in endless new contrivances of identity and political upheaval; but to my mother, this is no matter. She has stopped time through the incantation of her pacing, a trick to rival those of Merlin in Boorman's *Excalibur*.

Do you see her in her enormous blue poly-foam bathrobe? Do you see the pinkness of her cheeks? The wildness of her straw-yellow hair? The gleam of the tee-vee off the glasses on her face? This is her wizard's garb, and by the shuffle of her slippered feet and the repetition of millions of Hail Marys, the year shall forever be Nine-teen-Fifty-Eighty-Seventy-Four-Sixty-ish-Forty-Nine-Seventy-Two.

This is what I learned today: Her gynecologist was in the news for murdering his wife.

He did it while his teenaged daughter was at home. He was al-ready under criminal investigation for making fraudulent diagno-ses of his patients, which would mean he would make up a bunch of expensive tests for them to have, for ailments they didn't have, and then people like my mother would give bills to their insurance companies, and the insurance would refuse to pay them because the guy was under criminal investigation for fraud. So my mother stopped going to him, and a bunch of other patients stopped going to his palatial office of "rooms full of testing machines," and the guy eventually murders his wife "who everyone," my mother added, "said was such a nice lady."

My mother flashed back to when she sat with her legs spread on the stirrups—the most archaic and Spanish Inquisition-looking metallic scenario, in which a woman lays her feet on cold metal hooks, while the speculum, looking something like a cross between a can opener and a shoehorn, goes in and wrenches the cervix apart, and a rubber-gloved hand shoves in from here to Eternity. She said that this doctor, the one who murdered his wife, was "too rough" during his journeys through her cervix, his journeys to the very uterus that gave me life. (How does it feel? a male may ask. Like a tiny-tiny fraction of giving birth, and even a tiny fraction of labor isn't fun.)

I don't think I can claim any of my doctors have murdered their wives. Then again, I haven't been to a doctor since 2004.

This reminds me of that "news story" my mother was watching that was SPLATTERED ALL OVER THE TELEVISION the last time I visited her. It was about a husband who forced his beauty pageant wife to have so much life-threatening plastic surgery that she was incapacitated and died (suspiciously) on her pain meds. This story was broadcast about five times a day, kind of like an infomercial or like news that is REALLY IMPORTANT like stock market crashes and mass bee deaths, but no, this "news," specifically contrived to be like a horror movie with slowly floating montages of photos and creative "re-enactments" of the crime, it was shown on all of the programs my mother watches, every last unsolved-abduction-celebrity-make-over-mystery-suicide-drug-rehab-sex-change-ex-con-gigolo-juggalo-car-chase-call-in-with-your-problems-poison-pie-filling-nightmare show.

It was a story about another wife who everyone said was "just so nice, she couldn't hurt a fly." She was an ex-pageant winner and mother of adult children. She was under a sinister Svengali's spell and got surgeried to death for him.

My mother watches news stories like this all the time, which is probably why she was strangely nonplussed to hear her gynecologist was on trial for murder and trying to fake the evidence to make it look like his wife slipped on the bathroom floor. For shut-ins whose only sense of reality is what they get from the remaining "free" non-cable tee-vee channels, THIS IS LIVING.

The woman does not have a computer and I gave up showing her what to do when it took an hour to get her to use a mouse, which she still didn't understand. She has no greater portal to reality than a bunch of *Full House* reruns and forensic crime tee-vee shows where every ten minutes there is an autopsy, or a "crime of the heart." For millions of older women like her, sensational is the new norm, and the song "Hey Joe" is G-rated kiddie stuff: "And then I shot her...I shot her dead..."

No Knowns

THEN: THE QFC STOCKER who looks like Edgar Allan Poe is losing sleep. He has been losing sleep for years, but now he is growing perverse, starting to babble in the aisles, to seek refuge and companionship in the errant eyes of shoppers eyeballing the discount rack for vitamins and sugar-free blackberry jam. He is like a stray puppy, or a stray—raven. He said he lives in Tigard and commutes to this grocery store every night. That is something like a three-hour bus ride to and from his graveyard shift. He says he lives with his mother, and used to take a screenwriting class. He has watched hundreds of early-seventies films, and especially likes Brian DePalma. He still tries to write, but his life has become overwhelming. He lives with his mother, but there is SOMEONE ELSE in the house who throws knives. What kind of knives? How big? Does it matter? Poe shakes his head and looks spooked by how lost he has gotten in the memory of knives, and light bulbs, and mottled beige sofa cushions, and all the smells that make his mother's house what it is. It is an inventory of sensation, the life of this man, and perhaps in comparison to his room in the house of knives, the buzzing fluorescent lights and eternal night of satellite radio and the hauling of boxes are not as terrible as one would think. When he quits his job, I will never know what happens to him. I forget to ask his name.

NOW: He is gone—perhaps he has found work in a grocery store that isn't a three-hour bus ride away. I will wonder if he writes, if he gets more sleep, if his skin still looks like fine white dough made of rice flour.

I realize this means too many people. I only partially cared. I have no slug-trail, no scent, no knowns.

Catholic Schoolgirl

WHAT DOES IT MEAN to be a Catholic schoolgirl but realize there is a fetishization of the image of Catholic schoolgirls and one masturbates to the mirror image of one's junior-high plaid pleated skirt with nothing underneath from the perspective of a bearded truck driver from a CBS Movie of the Week because it is not enough to see yourself as sexy; there have to be OTHERS who uncontrollably move HANDS on PARTS; PRIVATE rumblings; SPLAT! What-DOES-it?? It means 1985.

Shiny New Products

THE OTHER NIGHT I WAS at a bar downtown that used to be an incredibly hip dance music place full of cocaine and competitive heroin-related skin rashes but now it is all dried up and the only thing that strip of downtown has to brag about anymore are meat markets with bondage swings where women who still wear "Daisy Dukes" with Uggs go to find party-men comprised of fluids: Party-man skin-sacs glisten in the half-light braised in a urinal cologne and on the inside a molecular substance composed of Chicken McNuggets, human sperm, carbon monoxide and a lifelike red formaldehyde courses in the place of blood.

This night was no exception. A friend of mine invited me to a DJ night but it was a Monday and the streets were deserted, the club barren except for a big-boned hipster bartender with artfully arranged fringe and a T-shirt that I think was meant to evoke a holographic fusion of James Franco and Steve Buscemi over his own body from the neck up. The room was emptyville, the skids, and not the fault of my DJ friend. It was raining, it was piddling and cold and no one's hearts were in the streets.

The theme was an "Italo-Disco" night but instead a gang of rowdy office people in expensive pajamas came in and requested hip-hop, a lot of hip-hop, but what they really wanted to hear (as my friend tried to dredge out any eighties stuff he had) was MODERN Top 40 stuff they could move their baggy limbs to. It was an office party full of young and muscular types with two older men who seemed to be overseers—spiritual coaches and miserly sadists if you will.

Everyone was dressed the same: The men had on baggy jeans with low waists, white sneakers. The men of color had baggier sweat-shirts with sports logos, while the whities had darker-color sweat-shirts, dark and unzipped to imply at times that they bench-press yet might contemplate the mysteries of life and death on rare occasions with Edgar Allan Poe's raven hovering by a nearby air duct in the office break room.

Most of the men wore baseball caps, and the women were equally sporty in their dress, but with tighter jeans and smaller sneakers. Two of the girls were disheveled in a way that indicated they hadn't embraced a militaristic femininity; only one, third crucial female with a punky bleach-blonde haircut and a breezy ever-smiling gait bounced in her tight jeans, wearing the finest bronzing products, and the combination of an immaculate haircut and a tomboy squint with the slightly bulging Hottentot gluteals that indicate a specific type of work on an exercise machine—she especially had the men of color easing into her personal space. This made one particular guy who was trying to look like an office Trent Reznor cringe with jealousy. At one point Trent even raced over to blondie and put her in a fake headlock. I overheard her say that her hometown was L.A.

Aha! A clue! It seemed they were still getting acquainted, this group. It HAD to be an office party. The more I watched the behavior of these twenty-somethings, the more they reminded me of college freshmen forced to perform at dormitory "mixers" or new recruits at an advertising agency having some enforced "social time" while the bosses (in camouflage "hip" pajamas) watch them to secretly take notes on which candidates, based on the nuances of drinking and flirting, will sink or swim.

As the beats went on, the office crew got more active. It was a mini-court of Nero in front of me full of men doing full frontal body-lunges at each other as if they were playing a football game. They would tackle each other, and then just as quickly tumble off, hopping away with a perfectly heterosexual nonchalance. Yep, just boys in the clubhouse making "ooo-oooo-ooogh" sounds as they pump fists and get into a sort of dancing circle, all the man-bodies jumping higher and higher like marionettes, and then spiraling away and winking and cracking knuckles and swigging black bottles and tumblers of whiskey and adjusting baseball caps before the next demonstration of swagger-stance.

There was a lot of competing for the L.A. blonde, and there was one guy of color who had a babyface and moves as sensual as the petals of a rose and he was just circulating around the room of fifteen office people grabbing each girl and bending her over to do doggie-style sex moves and each girl awkwardly obeyed and then without even looking at her face, he would slap each girl on the rear and move on. He demonstrated that he could have every one.

The girls tried all night to do doggie-style sex-submission moves on the guys, their bedenimmed posteriors aimlessly flying through the air in search of pantomime cock. I'm NOT JOKING. This seemed to be the only dance (other than the fake football huddle-marionette jump) that these people knew how to do. The two not-as-glam women gave up trying to offer their rear ends to the men, and so they disappeared to make out behind a column, secretly watching to see if the menfolk would notice because lesbianism is hot, ya know. One of the women was butch in an Italian way and almost COULD have been a lesbian or at least a volleyball star, while the clueless doe-faced one who kissed her was clearly just ready to kiss ANYONE for the illusion of an eyeblink's love; just a heartbeat please, just a heartbeat's worth of being worthy to live another day. Doe-face's rear end was tight and well-shaped in her jeans, it was a rear end barely out of high school, but her rear end could never survive the abuse of these weird sharks.

Gray-haired men with brush-cuts carefully watched and back-slapped the younger males. A lot of top-shelf whiskey was being poured. This MUST have been on a company's tab. Meat handled meat; men bent over women and slapped and thrust until the gesture lost all meaning; it had already lost its meaning before this night had even begun.

The two pseudo-lesbians returned to glow in front of the office men and offer their rear ends all over again. The dudes didn't notice.

Life is a clubhouse and everyone is a man, but some men have holes in front and don't get paid as much. Call it locker-room ethics, 101.

All I know is that something happened a long time ago, around the time when I was born and it created a dead generation. Money and care started leaving the public schools and cynicism became really hip in a way that nobody could shake and all of these children were raised that now have the bodies of adults but have no sense of history, or mystery, or life being comprised of more than a sort of wolfpack sense of regularity, and the impulse to have a shiny new product in one's hand; hell, to BE a shiny new product. THERE IS NOTHING MORE!

Bend over for the ultimate penetration, you shiny new products! For this pantomime cannot end in a time beyond history; a time beyond time.

Airports of Swift Ventilation and Candy-Scented Reveries

WHEN I WAS IN THE AIRPORT a couple weeks ago I saw many things of wonder and grace. I saw teenaged girls the height of hot air balloons with waists in black denim as thin as threads of licorice rope.

I saw a woman in a gray bun speaking nonstop about the importance of tracing one's genealogy as her husband, a red-faced man with a bushy moustache, gazed off to the horizon, to his lap, into a field of non-space while the woman rattled on to a healthy suburban family who could barely suppress giggles (ALL of them: Mama, Papa, and the Brussels-sprout babies with mall-hair, as if they walked out of an episode of some eighties sitcom).

And the old woman in her gray bun, she spoke of how the past was definitely far richer than the present. The past had Paul Revere and the *Mayflower*! (Well, I doubt she was thinking about Caligula and Attila the Hun.) The past was a world with vestal virgins and burning roots and the constant threat of smothering, of having the weight of the Ice Age or the Evil or *E. coli* and a dozen other forms of death catch up and force the trance of living to recede.

Yes, this flimsy filmy texture of consciousness; see it now? Hold it in your hands, and shake it real good. You can't shake it? I can't help you; I can only tell you I am similarly mesmerized by the ever-changing soda fountain voices of AWAKE until I am finally helpless and no more living can be had. BUT NOT YET! I can live, I can live! I have lungs and breathing, sincerely.

And on that note, I buzzed like a worker drone, jacked up on a caramel latte and too tired to really care about the things a person can BUY in the Newark airport, even though, like a World's Fair, it stretches on forever.

I felt a primal compulsion to check out the duty-free perfume store, but once I was in it, my huge suitcase was always in danger of knocking over crystalline displays of rainbow-hued ichors, and sales clerks, as bored as Persian cats, eyed my details, my lines, to determine if I was worth hustling. I had a disagreement with a lean and stone-cold Russian sales clerk about the scent of vanilla (I like it; she doesn't) and that pretty much ended our discussion. She realized she could not help me in the Vanilla Void.

And the more I stood under the spotlights, their range so narrow and precise, with my meaningless top-heavy suitcase, caffeinated blood pumping through my brain like some hastily huffed helium, I realized that I was as far from buying perfume as a human being could get.

Why the rush? Why do people in airports nervously shop at all? Does the monetary value of items (the more expensive, the better) guarantee that fate SIMPLY CANNOT ALLOW YOU TO DIE, because you have made so many investments in your future? Since when have Brookstone thirty-pressure-point jugular massage robots and ugly Missoni rip-off sweater-dresses made of scratchy plastic that feels like Easter straw and Sennheiser headphones and palm-sized Bose speakers and bobble-headed Ozzy dashboard companions and twelve bars of gourmet bacon chip chocolate from "single-source" suppliers and a small sterling silver cigarette holder embossed with Van Gogh's *Sunflowers* and an overpriced Beanie Baby meant to resemble one of Harry Potter's pet owls, and a small wand-like device that is meant to vibrate the blood vessels under one's arms to keep the muscle tone from getting all "turkey-flabby" under there for only four hundred dollars if you please, it is the latest in cellular vibration technology...

Since when did any of these novelties ward off death in a fiery plane crash, à la Buddy Holly and Amelia Earhart and all the others who sputtered out before planes became as safe as bassinets, right already?

It is hard to take off in a tin tub next to a kind nose-blowing lesbian couple and an elderly Wiccan Tank Girl and her ski-sweater son named Dylan—after Bob or Thomas I wonder?—and so many figments of pop cultural imagination giving off their restless muscle-fatigued fumes; their perfectly polished indecision; a carnal insouciance if you will, and NOT think about death.

But then once you are in the air, it is all excitement until twenty minutes passes and you realize you are really trapped for six hours with a full bladder or too much caffeine in your brain and even the book you brought to read is done an hour before touchdown, and the lights of every city in Nebraska and Montana make you think for a moment you are ten minutes away from the West Coast.

But the plane drags on, and you overhear the stupid dude covered in tattoos lecturing a sorority sister about the history of each tattoo that covers his HORRIBLY FLATULENT BODY in his painfully narcissistic surf voice while the mild-mannered guy in the faux-hawk, I mean the thirty-fifth mild-mannered guy on the plane to have some sort of experimental razor treatment on his scalp...

...he sits with the old couple from Bombay telling them about his graduate professor who spent an entire EIGHT MONTHS in India learning about classical stringed instruments and how eager the whippersnapper is and how endless his reverence for people in saffron and aqua robes because he will NEVER be as real, he can be NOTHING but a taffy cloud in the pitter-patter juggernaut of American Gum-Chew-Chew Grand-Theft-Auto-Mollyville.

And something about death and toxic gas from hungover red-eye dude-bros on planes and HOW COULD YOU letting it out right in the TSA shoe-removal aisle so that at least fifty of us shift our eyes like Nixon in your intestinal swill before its last embers die in the ventilation nation...

And should I have bought this sale perfume and that Murakami book wasn't what I expected but it makes me feel a snowy film of nostalgia anyway, about a Japan I never lived in, and a mad inventor, and the whiskey and wine he drinks, and I wouldn't have written that ending, but then again, why not? Oh God, I haven't slept for forty hours so when I get off the plane everyone in the airport will think I'm a drug mule or my real age and Thanks For the Memories... If I could LIVE in an airport, I swear to you I WOULD. I love airports; I love the constant motion; the varieties of human experience that are condensed into fifty-second glares. I love not having a life or a history or obligations for two seconds; I like being weightless and deathless yet treated like a sack of blood-covered cocaine by the TSA, YES.

I do love airports, and going forward, and feeling more real in the act of escape than I ever do at rest, YES.

Huck

AT THE BUS STOP I was caught in a gale-force blizzard of stink-ing-drunk computer programmers from Philadelphia who were here on business and a combination of alcohol and dislocation rendered them a bunch of snickering ten-year-old boys whose voices took on the tones of honking geese—that is, honking geese with very dry senses of humor. The youngest programmer, who unlike his cohorts was going for a boy-band Euro-pop look, tried hard to ply his wares on me as the bus rushed through the night and crossed the sinews of a rain-covered bridge.

Once I got downtown, I saw that the streets were deserted. A sleepy commuterless calm, like that inside an icebox, prevailed over the vacant remains of the city. As I walked toward my second bus stop, I noticed a figure behind me with a shambling gait. My periph-eral vision took him for a homeless dude or someone with nothing to get up to but mischief, and I kept my instincts aimed his way as I passed my bus stop and peered back.

He was a kid—he looked barely more than fifteen, and he had the rangy strut of a pro garbage-picker, a Brando without a brain. He started talking to me, and couldn't stop. It was dim, I am as they say "well-preserved," and despite being old enough to be his mother, he kept on going. He asked me if I was "partying" tonight and if I went to any bars and he even asked me what I had to drink. He spoke of traveling and wanting to get a raft and he showed me the huge assortment of knives in his pocket and told me he had spares in his bag coz he always needs to be equipped and he asked me where I was from and what I thought of buses and light rail trains and he loves grape-flavored Four Loko and there were many pauses, but I was kind to the kid—for he was a kid, getting excited when he asked if I had been to Disneyland. Asking me if I liked Eminem! (I politely told him I hadn't listened to enough Eminem to make up my mind) and his dad is a mechanic and he learned from him how to fix cars and street race and I told him he had a skill to last for life and he described getting into fights and the crack of one guy's arm in his hands and how he loves Disneyland! And he struck me as a cross between the Rain Man and Huck Finn, this strange rural rap boy with his boy-band face and his need to be a homicidal party machine.

He must be equipped...and he must be a man...and he must mention all the flavors of drinks he likes ONE MORE TIME, and when the bus finally came, we sat in different seats and he kept in his shy yet bubbly way trying to say more but I ended up looking out a window and he checked his phone and told a person at a party destination he was on his way and then proceeded, like a puppy, to latch on to two hip educated people sitting behind him by talking about Four Loko grape flavor and the number of Jello shots he drank in a night and showing them where his thumb was cut off "clean" and sewn back on. He had a new family, this oily boy who reminded me of a muscular shaved seal.

This boy, this boy who feels like French fries and nylon jerseys, a boy made out of instant lemonade crystals and gruntwork genes. I saw him looking at my eyes in the reflection of the glass, his soap-bubble squint superimposed over the shifting buildings, the strip club, the dog food factory, the empty streets. When I got off at my stop, I wished him good luck in his travels (he was intent on going to Wisconsin and "Huntington Beach" for some reason) and the rude aluminum tube ferried him on, like it ferries everyone on, to their unique and isolated fates.

Superball Sunday

I JUST TALKED TO MY MOTHER on the phone and she was telling me more about the neighbor who got killed. This story is true; there are clippings to prove it. So her neighbor was a real strutting greaser guy (this is New York, see) right out of a Springsteen song and he used to have parties all night and his kids (according to my mother) look like they're starving and his wife really keeps to herself after someone broke into his house and shot him dead. My mother heard the shots and everything. She thought it might have been thunder or a garbage truck; but now—the stuff of her paranoid dreams has actually happened within a hundred feet of her.

I love her descriptions of how the guy used to look, with his ponytail and his puffed-up leather jacket, walking down the street on summer days like he had just won a prizefight, like Putin, like any mob boss, showing the street who was king of the hill.

Today my mother said she was worried about his family accidentally getting our mail, opening it, pasting it shut again, and returning it a month later. According to her this has happened several times, and the worst was when it happened with a box of chocolates left in the snow for three days. She went on about how the kids are starving yet the trash is always piled really full, several 64-gallon loads of it.

What could this family be throwing away? Is any of it food waste, my mother wonders? She doesn't see the kids outside very much, and the mother looks beaten down. Yet, as she added, there was a SUPERBALL SUNDAY party earlier in the year and cars lined the street going into the house of BLOOD.

My mother said SUPERBALL SUNDAY many times so I know it wasn't a slip of the lip. The idea of a woman so far outside the world of men that she calls this date Superball Sunday gives me a warm glow inside. As for my mother being so close to a murder, I'm not actually worried. Whatever is going on with that family has to do with ties to a world my mother does not and will never inhabit, the proof of which is her usage of the word Superball.

Pinky

A MAN STRUTS OUT OF the past with a proud Mayan face, frizzy ponytail, a dog barely larger than a mouse: The man moves, a don't-fuck-with-me dance in baggy blue jeans and a leather bomber jacket. His body punches forward on the concrete...it is as if his face, arms, and feet are boxing gloves, not flesh. At a traffic light the man slows. He smiles. The dog is on a long leash and wears a waterproof pink apron.

Reminders of a Lifetime Ago

ON THE BUS AN OBESE WOMAN with the face of Sarah Silverman huddled in a postal worker's jacket though I do not think she was a postal worker. She peered into a hardcover library book, its cover featuring shattered crystals on a deep blue field; a book which looked conspicuously like a romance. Though her hair was untouched by gray, she clearly was on her way to an early-stage hunchback, the sort writers, composers, and factory workers get by the age of thirty-five from decades of leaning over things which deform a body with an inner passion, a smelting-hot perversity. Her face was buried, bird-like, in the pages of that book. The bus could have been on fire for all it mattered. Her legs, so thick and unhealthy-looking, and capped by sensible office pumps, reminded me of Margaret Thatcher, a thousand Margaret Thatchers—the women of my childhood TV experience.

As I gawked at her, the same way a man in hiking gear was gawking at me, I caught a shadow on the reader's forehead. I thought it would be fitting if a woman so outside of "hip and happening" human patterns also had a large black mole on her face, but as I watched further, the angle of her profile shifted so slightly and I saw that it was a large cross made of ash.

OF COURSE! It is the beginning of Lent (for diligent Catholics everywhere) and those who can maintain the belief in such things have flocked to their churches today to get ash-crosses placed on their foreheads to symbolize what will be several weeks of sacrifice—of fish, of fowl, of gambling, of sex, of video games; you name it, Catholics are supposed to be sacrificing SOMETHING right now. Last night was the last hurrah, Mardi Gras, before the plenty of Easter arrives. I wonder if the Earth can give up global warming until Easter, too. Probably not.

The deal is that I was raised by two extremely Polish-Catholic women and so I have memories of this Ash Wednesday routine. The way EVERY kid in our heavily Catholic neighborhood would have these ashes on his or her face, and you were supposed to be respectful of them, like God IT-SELF was having a beach-blanket siesta on your forehead and YOU MUST NOT WIPE THOSE ASHES OFF or you would be a heathen, bub!

Of course I, being a vain kid who thought the ashes in no way looked good on my face, had a way of slowly but surely grazing my hands against the ash-cross all day, wiping the forehead clean at a pace that could only be studied under time-lapse photography. Any ashes that went on at 11 a.m. would seem like only a faint WISP— perhaps a trick of the light—by 4 p.m., and I would come home from church or school not seeming like a conspicuous fool.

See, it was always the clueless kids who kept the rich black smear on all day, looking like the lemmings they were—the ones who would join the army, or believe in Santa Claus, or laugh at stupid jokes; the kids who took an extra two minutes to figure out the difference between AM and PM; the kids who would never understand birth control.

That ash woman may still be on the bus, racing through another crystal-coated romance, perhaps her third of the day. Beneath her ashes and her weight is a supermodel's face. I wondered if in her youth she was ever molested. I wondered if anyone other than myself saw the genetic gifts she had that were now covered by several layers of fantasy and an inexplicable postal worker's rain-tarp.

Tonight, as the bus zoomed down the hill past Powell and 42nd, I saw a packed parking lot of cars, everyone appearing to leave an event at the same time. I wondered if it was a game, or a show, or just a hot night at the bowling alley, but then I saw that the squat building with its mass headlight exodus was a church.

A CHURCH, mind you! People still GO to those!!! At least a hundred people covered in ashes were spilling out, getting in their cars, and ultimately not showing their ashes to the world. Soon those drivers' ashes would be in hot showers; asleep in beds. Most ash-people move smoothly from daylight institutions to locomotion-pods to their sleep-coffins these days.

Lent...it is kind of like scented erasers and graham crackers, something I haven't thought of since I was a child; and THAT, my friends, was a lifetime ago.

Free Ride

IS HE A JUNKIE which led to his injuries? Or is he on pain meds? Which came first—the chicken or the egg? A guy gets on the bus, a pauper in a gray cotton sweatsuit. Beneath the loose fabric, he is emaciated, may have one arm missing, or a Thalidomide stump concealed on his left-hand side. His face and hair make him a dead ringer for Mickey Rourke in the movie *Barfly*. His features are tender, yet bullish. His voice is nearly gone as he hauls a nonelectric wheelchair up the steps and begs for a free ride. The driver says yes. The guy gets settled and starts nodding off, over and over again. I notice his right sweatpants leg is stuffed with bloody rags that have leaked out and are now wet with rain. He is a stuffed animal leaking its innards, gauze, strips of cotton. He could be thirty-three or forty-five, who knows? I see a brown pharmacy bag on the seat of his wheelchair. He nods: Up, down, up, down. There is a beauty to what he once was. It stuns me. I imagine kissing him. I start talking to myself: "He's beautiful, he's beautiful—but he's not."

Plant Abduction

THIS IS A STRANGE STORY about motherlessness.

I was twenty-three years old and living in the yellow brick building named "The Cambrian," occupying the same hall as the operatic schizophrenic Romanian; she had a name that ended in a U and frequently screamed at the top of her lungs to pets and children who were not really there. She looked like she was made of overbaked sugar paste, and her hair, in a black helmet of pin curls, suited the severity of her body, her bustline (a bosom of such heaving proportions!) reined in by a harness so vast and precise that each breast was molded into a cone shape and aimed straight ahead, like missiles of womanly madness from a mother who rebelled against her young.

I frame this story with her, the battleship. She, who resembled a bull. She, who was a living Diane Arbus photograph. Upon my moving to Portland, she was one of the first people I really took notice of, dragging her feet in sensible brown loafers outside the Nordstrom's department store, an oversized sixties leopard-print coat masking her frame and giving even more of the impression that she, like an anomaly of physics, existed as a super-hot, super-densely concentrated mass. She clutched a small black handbag to her chest and looked at the face of each passerby as if we were phantoms.

Does anyone remember the guy who dressed in sweatpants and topped it all off with an oversized banana split of a wig and a Tammy Faye Bakker application of makeup? These two belong together in my mind's eye.

But anyway, this is not about urban bizarros; this is about the abduction of a plant accompanied by a ludicrously "hip" art statement.

On the first floor of The Cambrian a young Hispanic woman lived with a very old woman, who may have been her grandmother. The end of their hall was very dim. There were no windows in these halls. The walls were covered in poo-brown wood paneling, and the doors were painted black. The fluorescent bulbs installed every few doors down cast just enough light to put one's key in a lock and swing wide.

One day, upon entering the building, I noticed an enormous plant outside of this lady's door. It sat on an expensive-looking stand painted bronze. The stand was made of curlicues of metal which made deep and resonant pings when I thumped them with my hands. It was very mythological-looking, this plant stand.

The plant itself was the sort that I often mistake for fake plants. You know the kind: It looks like seaweed and uncooked pasta, and plastic. It feels waxy to the touch. You caress one of its fronds and still can't figure out whether it is a living plant or a fake.

After much inspection, I decided that it was a real plant.

I ended up entering and leaving the building every day, and couldn't stop thinking about this plant left in the darkness at the end of the hall. One day, I decided to take action.

In flowery script, I wrote a note that was FROM the plant and taped it to the plant.

"HELP! I need light! Please take me inside and put me next to a window. Sincerely, Your Plant"

The note remained taped to the plant for several days, but one day it was finally removed.

No one had dragged the heavy plant stand with its occupant inside.

Maybe it was a gift that neither the girl or her grandmother wanted. Maybe they were too busy struggling to make money to care. Maybe the grandmother was dying, and it was just too much stress for the young woman to think about a stupid plant. Maybe they didn't speak a word of English and didn't understand my note. I simply didn't know.

So after waiting a decent amount of time, I stole the plant.

The plant and its stand were heavy. It should be obvious to you by now that I was enamored with the plant stand; the plant, however, looked so unreal, so unyielding, that it was hard for me to care about its fate.

I watered it and put it next to a window. Days passed. Try as I might, it was just not the sort of plant I could anthropomorphize or find aesthetic pleasure in possessing. All I had done was provide it light, which I...think it needed.

I and my boyfriend of the time dressed up in ridiculous Patty Hearst-style hippie-military garb and held a toy gun, posing for pictures with the "liberated" plant. In our pictures, the plant was wearing a ransom note.

I gave the ugly plant to this boyfriend, and kept the mythological and expensive-looking stand.

I never figured out what I could keep in the plant stand other than a plant, and eventually gave it away, as well.

I am thinking about it because I have a plant I want to put in a plant stand and wish I still had that crazy heavy bronze monstrosity.

It was an impressive-looking plant stand. It had class—even if I didn't.

Amtrak and the Golden Showers

I WAS TWENTY-SEVEN YEARS OLD and in a relationship with a nine-teen-year-old acid freak who called me his sugar mama and he said I was in all categories "okay" and I was about to have a book published and I was high on life and everyone I was close to was suicidal or just really, really old. One month I was short on rent money and this guy who was a well-known album-cover artist downtown, he had an apartment with tinfoil-taped windows for real, well we went to a diner and he said "I'll give you fifteen dollars if you give me a blowjob." This was in the Roxy. It's the sort of thing that is supposed to be said in the Roxy, in my opinion, but you know, fifteen dollars isn't enough for my services and I declined this pathetic thing that couldn't really even be called an offer so much as a stab in the dark. The deal is that I am going to talk about Steve Perry, the lead singer of the band Journey. For the kiddies out there, this is the band that sings "Don't Stop Believing"—a song usually gargled by walruses from the innards of every karaoke joint from coast to coast of our fair nation; a song that should probably be our National Anthem.

While dating this guy who said I was kind of okay, well, yeah I was obsessed with him because I thought he was an Adonis, and he did writing as dark as my own, and yet he didn't care for mine because mine was too "fictional" and he wanted sex, gore, and drugs mainline-raw-spit-spit-choke-chokehold without all that emotional stuff I tended to add to my work...so I was dating him, this tall hu-man Warner Brothers pussycat of a man, a man who didn't take things "straight" as the Jonathan Richman song goes, and I was on the Amtrak train. I was taking my once-a-year trip to New York to visit my mother and grandmother. I looked like a street urchin. I wore this enormous gas station attendant's jacket and combat boots and a lot of mascara and I was just coming back from New York to get to Portland when the train stopped on the tracks, right outside of Chicago.

The train was stuck on the tracks for hours. I had work to get back to in Portland, and I was going to miss it. I needed to make phone calls. Only drug dealers and CEOs had cell phones at this time. I had to let my impatience dissolve and accept the beer and camaraderie of a gaggle of party people on the train. I always meet the party people on the train. My mascara tells them to sit near me. My mascara tells them that life is but a dream.

These party people, I remember them well. There was a squat Latina woman with shaved eyebrows, and what she had in their place were these two perfect arches that reminded me of the brows of Divine. She was rounded in a way that promises dark enchanted secrets for a week and she was old before her time. There was a tall guy from Louisiana who spoke in such a thick accent I could barely understand every second word he said. He looked like a cigarette butt, a busted violin; he had shadows under his eyes, and shorn black hair. The guy was haunted, just occupying space. There was a blond guy from California who said he had a friend who had a friend who worked in a brothel in L.A. This friend of a friend had Steve Perry come in. Steve Perry liked golden showers!

One of the gang didn't know what golden showers were, and so the rest of us explained it to him. I don't remember all the people in the gang. All I know is that we were put up, courtesy of Amtrak, in a posh Chicago hotel. Well, it was posh for what we were used to at the time. Over several hours of the night, I watched the drinkers pair off, and I retired to my own room, glad to have a break from the gaiety and glad to stop being an imposter, a floating balloon-head.

I have told this Steve Perry story many times, whenever someone plays a Journey song, I think. I don't care if it is true or not; it is just a memory I savor like an elderly woman taking a dried rose petal out of a keepsake box. She caresses her Steve Perry Golden Shower story with affectionate fingers. For this is one of the building blocks of my identity, as surely as an amino acid twists into the elegant architecture of my DNA.

Other Candy

I PRIDE MYSELF IN my feel of a face; before she was a tweaker, the woman with the black hair and the tattered business blazer was Irish. Along with her boyfriend, a beet-red weasel in desert army boots covered in mud, she hauled bags of bottles into the midnight supermarket, scavenged presumably from the same place the couple had scavenged the upended oven, coils of wire, boxes, and dented who-knows-what sort of trash piled in a nest, piled like a spaceship made of junk on top of the pickup truck. The man waited for a clerk (one of several teenaged stoned dudes listening to satellite emo) while the woman kneeled before a candy display whispering words, words that wove and gnawed at the air like her nails now gnawed at the blisters on her face. She was once cheerleader-pretty, probably five, ten years ago. The business checks of her jacket told me she was still trying to be. She got up from kneeling and said out loud, "Where's the rest of the candy??" I pointed to half an aisle of candy, more candy than anyone could name or dream of. "Not that!" she muttered to the floor. "I want OTHER candy..."

Whiskers

WHEN I WAS THIRTY-THREE years old I was breaking up with a junkie whom I dated for four years. I tried to break up many times, but breaking up is hard to do. During one of the spells that we were broken up, my cat Baby was hit by a van. I was living downtown and a squatter-girl saw it happen. In a moment that could be from a made-for-tee-vee special, the squatter-girl picked up Baby's limp and bleeding black body from the curb and started crying at the passing traffic. She was bawling her eyes out and cradling Baby in her arms, and trying to hail someone to stop.

A blonde well-coiffed woman in a power suit driving a convertible came to her aid and the two of them drove Baby to DoveLewis Hospital, where Baby got free treatment. Baby had a limp and nerve damage, but bounced back in a few months, being a petite acrobat with a strong will to live. And yes, this has to do with junkies. I'll tell you how.

During one of the times my boyfriend and I were broken up—let's call him Chris—he told me he wanted to quit drugs. He also told me I was fat, that my friends secretly hated me, and that he was starting to have affairs with AIDS patients in the Rose Garden who begged him for sex and licked his ears. So perhaps we could say that he was not the most reliable witness, for anything—but the deal is, he was a talented writer and I was still in many ways attached to what he was, and what he could have been.

I remember one morning when Chris was getting intolerable. He showed up at my apartment in heavy withdrawals, and he saw that I had been eating a chocolate bar. He started rolling on the floor and whining that he was dying and yes, that if I didn't give him some of my chocolate bar, he WOULD die. Picture a guy with the head of Henry Rollins and the body of a longshoreman gone to pot, and place it in cheap Costco clothing that his father threw at him like a number of sad black garbage bags, and now place random drawings, safety pins and scrawled messages on top of this business, and you can picture what I am saying.

I ended up calling Chris' mother, something I wouldn't normally do for any grown adult, because he needed some sort of treatment, or at the very least to be taken out of my room.

His mother and I drove him to his apartment, where we proceeded to clean it and return everything to an amazing hotel standard of livability before he could mess it up again with the detritus of burned tinfoil, cigarette butts and sweaty rags.

Toward the end of my knowing Chris, he told me that he really wanted to quit pills and heroin and that he needed me to hide his drugs in MY apartment.

So he gave me the drugs to hide and told me to never give them to him, no matter how much he begged me. Or at the least, only dole out a small amount if it seemed that he was suffering too much.

Of course I was skeptical about the entire enterprise, but I hid this pile of pills and miscellany in a sock in a suitcase on the highest shelf in the back of my closet and waited for the inevitable.

Which happened. At about three a.m....and kept happening until five a.m....until I got sick of the man buzzing my buzzer and calling my phone and throwing things at the side of my building, and I gave him his drugs and let him go.

Of course I didn't really let him go until he pulled a knife on me in my apartment. That's when I REALLY let him go, for good, and NEVER took him back.

Having a knife held at you for ten minutes is truly a video-game moment. Your entire body and mind unite, become crystal-clear. You realize that you are acting FOR KEEPS and you are very careful in your words and motions in ways you never have been before.

It took me a while to talk this man into putting down the knife, and convincing him (extremely high on MANY substances) that if he waited for me outside, I would come with him to his apartment to borrow a book.

The minute he was outside of the building I didn't let him back in. It took me about an hour to make the decision to call the cops. It took me an hour to realize what had happened and that it could happen again.

I remember being in the courthouse nine to five the next day, on very little sleep, with a room full of mostly women waiting to complete the paperwork to file against angry men. To clarify whose paperwork was being dealt with, the clerk would hold up each man's mugshot to the crowd of women. When the clerk held up mine, a photograph of a wasted-looking black-eyed man who looked like Henry Rollins given the steamroller treatment, the women in the room all cringed and went, "Ooooh! Good thing he's in HERE now!"

That made me a little amused. I can't tell you exactly why, but if this man made a whole room of battered women happy that someone that scary-looking was behind bars for even a moment, I, as conflicted as I was about protecting myself, knew I had done something right.

Of course, looks aren't everything. And I don't usually agree with the choir.

I bring up my cat and junkies for this reason. I have known a lot of addicts, and loved a lot of addicts in my life, and I stupidly believed at moments that my love could change them—that they would ACTUALLY CHOOSE LOVE over drugs, over the pleasure and security they felt in fairly predictable medications. What a fool I have sometimes been!

I remember being with Chris, during the end days, when he was begging me to help him quit, and I held up one of Baby's whiskers, a sturdy black tapered silhouette of a whisker, and I twiddled it in my hand, and gave it to Chris to put inside his wallet.

I said, "Think of what a survivor Baby is. Think of her strength. Think of the odds of her surviving being hit by a van! If Baby can make it, so can you. Whenever you feel the urge to give in, think of Baby. Take this whisker out of your wallet and hold it, and think of Baby."

Many years have passed and Baby is dying now. She is fifteen years old and has kidney disease. She is still a survivor, but every week she goes through more changes, the changes a body undergoes on the path to death.

I never willingly throw away cat whiskers. I have small piles of them collected all over my house—enough Baby whiskers to assist an entire ward of junkies going cold turkey. Or alcoholics. Or those who are used to being alone. Or those who are afraid of change. Or those who want to kill their brains. Or those who cannot get over everything.

I have so many cat whiskers, and I cannot give them to anyone, because I know that I and my whiskers have no power to change anyone but myself.

The Traces of Byzantium

MASTURBATION MEMORY NUMBER 2: It was a humid summer night in Syracuse, New York. The neighborhood was full of elderly Polish couples who would slowly drop like flies; flies behind votive candles, sacred hearts; copper domes, the traces of Byzantium. I lived with my grandparents. The backyard was overgrown by trees. I opened my window as high as it would go, pinned the curtains back. I got a facecloth and slowly sponged my body, pressing as close to the window as I could go without breaking the screen that kept the mosquitos out, hoping someone, some elderly Polish man might be peering out a window and notice my naked body. It was eleven-thirty at night. No old Polish men would be awake at this point, so I imagined that a vagrant or maybe a cat burglar might come along instead. I was thirteen.

Stollingdenturemouth

AFTER COMPLAINING ABOUT WAITING for buses I should redeem myself or freshen the air or wave a magic wand of words by telling you some highlights of the bus life tonight: There was a tag-team of party babes, both whom I imagine were pushing forty and showing it in their distinct ways. The one on the left had no teeth; I mean NO teeth, and she was not ashamed of this scenario. Her hair was freshly bleached white with streaks of a lovely lilac color in the front (I always boggle at how women who are made of drugs can grow better hair than me—someone once told me I was doomed to have hair as fine as cobwebs because I was Polish) and this woman had a face like an Appalachian gas station attendant and a flirty little tank top with khaki shorts and the sort of tan that comes from spending long hours in the sun and she was leaning toward her friend with a sense of mastery, the way her legs were so casually spread, and she smiled and licked her lips, smile and lick and smile and lick repeatedly, as if her lips were actually made of the caramelized sugar in a lollipop. Her smile was not quite a smile so much as a portal, a crease in reality as we know it, through which one small enough might travel to another dimension where Carl Stalling songs play nonstop and Bugs Bunny finally reveals what he was getting at all those times he dressed in drag. Her friend had a frightened face, like a Diane Keaton without the confidence to wear menswear on a daily basis, and the friend nervously tap-tap-tapped her rhinestone-crusted sandal up and down exhibiting what we these diagnosis-themed days call "Restless Leg Syndrome" and the rest of the non-Diane's leg was pale and very exposed all the way up to a tattoo of a heart with some guy's name on it way-way up at the edge of the short-short khakis where say her hip bone was about to begin. I wanted the non-Diane to calm down but she kept peeking at me and looking worried and trying to smile with her friend and she was drunk, and she needed to be drunk and I don't know where she came from or where she would go with her troubled Welsh eyes and her shaking-shaking foot and all of that non-Diane thigh flesh shown to all of us forever and ever in this bus-chamber in some conceptual realm where we will always be together...

...how I love the party women, I repeat, and how we all look at each other with a mixture of envy and stress and dread of how we will all make ends meet and deal with the ticking time.

A Baby for the People

MY MOTHER ON THE PHONE:

"I'm worried because time passes and I'm worried because the pattern of the weather and I'm worried because you have to be you. Judge Judy said a woman has to protect herself. She has a limited time to make a success of herself and look good. She said men have revivals. A man has to have several professions and he meets many women over the years and a woman doesn't have that. You have to take care of your health."

Then she went on to describe to me the Christmas cards she bought, several only for me, and asked me which one she should send. She told me that as a "preemie" I still looked like a newborn when I was one year old. She said I was long and skinny and hats fell over my nose and a bottle of baby formula broke on my face and it made me laugh hysterically, which made all of the adults in the room laugh hysterically. Her words:

"You were a baby for people. You liked to be around people. There were many ads on tee-vee you liked. There was one cola ad on tee-vee for a cola that doesn't exist anymore. When it came on you would point to me to pick you up and I was supposed to sway you back and forth. You would move your toes in time to the jingle. You had an excellent sense of rhythm. You swayed your feet to cola commercials and pointed your toes like a ballerina. Do you remember your heated plate?"

Now she is talking about everything she learned from reading Tori Spelling's autobiography. She has learned that not everyone understands the "megawealthy."

A Terminal Case

THERE'S A GUY DRESSED LIKE a Roma cab driver from London in the early nineties pacing back and forth in slow motion at the bus stop—shambling gait, scrawny torso and toothpick legs in black jeans. His oversized white blouse is half in and out of a brown wool vest and the cap on his head is perfectly coordinated with a terminal case of pussyface—you know, the condition men have where they grow enlarged goatees that circle their lips like the letter "O"—as in "Oh, no! Another guy who took it upon himself to go into the field of chin creation, or re-masculation, or looking like a white guy's idea of what black is"—and anyway, he seems to have been at this bus stop for well over an hour, maybe two, pacing and smoking his cigarettes, all twenty-seven years of him. If Frank Sinatra were alive now and twenty-seven, would he have pussyface too? All I know is this dishwasher-hand hornet-eyed wilde childe from a Pogues video does not seem to be getting on a bus. He is intimately connected to the profound stone garbage can—perhaps married to it. Has he been paid to collect data on me? Can he see that I am wearing an ancient pair of glasses that make me look like a librarian and how are his combat boots doing and when was the last time he changed his underwear? Does he live on cold pizza? Is he waiting for the bus that takes him to another galaxy? His buttocks tell the fortune of manhole covers. The sidewalk cracks have great futures. On a dark and stormy night I will meet a soul-covered windowpane, bite the big Grecian Formula and we call this The Sun.

Calling Hours

AT MY GRANDMOTHER'S CALLING HOURS very few people came and the funeral director nervously sat with his wide thin mouth set in a Polish jaw, and perfectly brilliantined Alfalfa hair, and all of this installed in a trim black suit that made him all angle, all body, and he was a strange one, as funeral directors are.

Four people came. We were sitting in a room for two hours and four people came. Half of this sum consisted of an old couple from church who sat near my grandmother's pew and they spent ten minutes talking about their health problems. They were a tiny Italian couple, like voodoo gimlets made of chicken wings and twine. Put wigs on top, and voiceboxes in their throats—and voilà! You have autopilot humanity.

I think that this pair only came to see what the body looked like dead. The woman said that she had wrecked her kidneys from taking prednisone for some ailment that was not relevant to me or my mother and definitely not to my grandmother's corpse done up like Liberace in the corner.

There was a blue cast to my grandmother's lips that someone had tried to cover up with makeup. Her hair was done, and her hands were folded, a gesture that does not call to mind the state a person is in after a bypass operation fails to "take." Women who are eighty-six should generally not have bypass operations. We do not live in the future yet, and this rate, maybe we never will.

My grandmother's lawyer came. The lawyer was a woman none of us wanted to know, a neighborhood creep who tried to sniff out anyone about to die so she could "rewrite wills" and get herself as-signed as a benefactor for having done all of this work. This lawyer was so crooked, and yet so sexy. She was a tidy blonde with an easy barstool laugh and eyes that studied everything. She complained during the visit that she was ruining her weekend plans by having to show up at a funeral. She said this with her easy barstool laugh, and proceeded to make bank.

My grandmother's dentist came. He was a man named Vincent with wide hazel eyes set in a milk chocolate face and he seemed, like many old Italian men, to be sculpted out of marzipan, down to the fine gray and black hairs of his widow's peak. He offered sincere, emotionally impressive condolences, as if he had experienced an intimate relationship with my grandmother, rather than having only polished her teeth for a handful of years.

And that was that. There were many gaps where I, like a prisoner in a cell, repeated my steps, my circuit around the room to where my grandmother was on display.

The funeral director had apparently never done a service for a shut-in before. He was getting increasingly nervous as the min-utes ticked past. He felt like he needed to say something, or offer something to my mother and me, as a substitute for the potential mourners who would never come. And so he did the most bizarre thing you could imagine.

He told a story that seemed engineered to make us feel even worse.

I can tell that he meant well. He was just somewhat...simple. Making us feel bad was not his intention. This is what he said:

He said that he will never forget the funeral of the doctor who committed suicide.

See him now: That wide jaw, those dark eyes, the stringy black hair in an extreme combover that made a man pushing fifty look more like a trophy pulled from an Egyptian tomb.

You remember the Doctor? Oh, everyone must remember the Doctor! He worked up at Community General. He spent many years in the emergency room and he got really involved with his patients. He would go on house calls and check up on each patient long after they had passed out of his immediate care. He worked so hard, he seemed to go without sleep to get his license at twenty-six and he started a family and had a beautiful house and these children he gave everything to.

You know, he often took on charity cases? If people couldn't pay, he'd say, that's okay, brother, and he'd say, you're a baker, just bring me some bread sometime, or you're a musician, just bring me one of your CDs when you can make it by.

He was so good, not a mean bone in his body. Man, this man was made of love, which is why it was such a shock when they found him in his bathtub. He had slit his wrists, and drifted off.

They figured he had been "gone" for several hours before the body was found. Of course this is a terrible, traumatic thing for a family to come home to, the funeral director said, and everyone was saddened and confused, and didn't have any clue that the Doctor was going through so much pain. Why couldn't he have spoken to anyone of his pain?

Maybe, I thought to myself, because he knew that no one, not even a doctor, can heal the deeper, inner pain.

And if you speak of a pain that cannot be healed by anyone else, what can people really do with it?

It just sits there in the air like the fume of a pool of vomit, like my armpit, like the way I feel tonight.

And oh, you wouldn't believe it, the funeral director said, we had to extend the calling hours! This Doctor, you could not even begin to imagine how one man could touch so many lives! You see that Burger King down there? There were cars backed up to Carvel cakes and down to the Dunkin' Donuts. There were hundreds of people making two loops around the block, trying to get in to calling hours!

We couldn't count them all. We ran out of programs. It was so special, so very special. The Doctor had touched so many people.

And yet, I thought to myself, he was dead, as dead as dead can be.

My mother appeared to be absorbed in the funeral director's story, as she would be in any Movie of the Week. It was a story, all right: It had death, it had the mystery behind the death, and it had the lives changed by the death. Isn't that what people look for in their popular entertainment?

After calling hours, my grandmother's casket was closed and put in the hearse, driven to a nearby church, where a nun sang her rendition of "Ave Maria."

Now I know that I say "singing like a nun" as an insult most of the time, but this nun, she had a powerful voice. Tears came out of my eyes as I stared at the empty church.

There was supposed to be a "reception" in the church basement, kind of like a wake. There was a long table with a paper cloth on it covered in chocolate chip brownies, cupcakes, some sort of green bean casserole, and plastic cups in which one could pour Kool-Aid or Diet Pepsi from a couple of two-liter bottles that sat under the fluorescent lights, smooth and impermeable, like dolphins.

No one we knew was in this room. My family had no real friends. I think even the old ladies who were part of an anonymous church bake-committee were equally perplexed as to why they had made all of this sugary crap, I mean tins and pans and platters of total candy-coated garbage whipped from mixes and poured in molds and thickened by sawdust and horse hooves, and no one was here to eat it!

Several folding tables spanned across the room, and a woman from the funeral home, the director's assistant, a blonde middle-aged cutie in black, she sat with us so that it would not literally be two people, my mother and I, in an empty room.

The funeral director's assistant was nervous, as well, but not as nervous as her employer. She started telling us a long and involved tale of how she was working in the funeral home and tripped on the stairs and didn't have much feeling in her leg. She had a blood clot, and then some exploratory surgery where a small tube with a microscopic camera on the end was placed in her arteries to explore the blood clot but this actually caused more blood clots and she almost died of an aneurysm in her head that connected with all of this.

Here I was, a thirty-three-year-old staring at this woman who looked like a relatively fit and flirty forty-five but she had all of these nightmare tales of her body falling apart that I would have never guessed if she wasn't just spilling them on the table to take the place of the untouched cupcake I grabbed out of politeness, and nothing more.

Everyone killed time, until it was time to take the long drive out to the cemetery, which was beyond the city limits.

The ground was covered in thick layers of snow and ice. I was wearing a waterproof pair of sixties go-go boots made of a thin vinyl and as I stood there at the edge of my grandmother's grave, the cold of the ice, of the Earth itself, started overtaking my feet, making them numb, and traveling up my legs.

The ground itself that was about to receive my grandmother's body was showing me what it was made of. Good God, I already thought about death all the time, and now the Earth, itself, was arranging a meet-and-greet!

My grandfather's body was already down there. The two people who raised me were now equally dead, and their bones would rest together in caskets with satin pillows turned yellow and pink and Lord knows what other psychedelic colors bodies and caskets turn, a rainbow of colors, when the embalming fluid expires.

I wondered what my grandfather's dead face, already under the ground for eight years, looked like. Was it covered in a fuzzy white mold? What parts had collapsed? What a farce he would think the whole thing to be, were he able to watch his body rot on satin pillows!

He only cared about electricity and his family, and sometimes when he sat under a tree in the backyard smoking his weekend cigar, he said the sun was beautiful, and the birds sounded beautiful, too.

Now my grandmother was about to join the satin-casket ranks of the moldy, the THINGS. The ice would keep her looking fresh for a while.

Was the Doctor here, too? Would my mother one day be here? I didn't want to be.

Don't bury me anywhere. Don't replace my blood with a lifelike fluid. I know too much and I care too little about satin pillows. All that matters to me is what we do with the NOW.

Chew Toy and Thor

ON THE BUS YESTERDAY were two barfly lovers, lovers who ARE the living embodiment of alcohol, and the living embodiment of America. As the bus ride progressed, I drank in their body language, as if I were licking it from their every pore. The man was a brawny man, sunburnt to a perfect crab color, and his long yellow hair was a mantle of light to rival that of Axl Rose in his prime. Both he and his lady friend were in tank tops. The lady is of the type I call "Chew Toy"—the sort of stout middle-aged woman who has spent so many hours of her life drinking, smoking, and getting into domestic abuse cases with men that she starts to resemble one of those felt toys with whiskers that a dog has been carrying in its mouth for three years, idly tearing off bits of syntha-flesh to expose the matted gray stuffing underneath. Her frizz of brown hair was knotted in a bun, with a bandanna headband adding to her summery style. They leaned into each other's shoulders like two wax candles melting on a windowsill. Thor (I will call him Thor, because he felt like a Norse god gone astray) tenderly kissed Chew Toy's neck. They leaned into each other's ears, loudly whispering and cackling with the conspiratorial quality that people have when they know they are going to be on a long drunk and THE ENTIRE PLANET is a playground, and every public park is a bed, and every MOMENT the COSMOS is opening up and about to deliver oral sex and beef jerky. And I am not saying this lightly. I know that when I am in the presence of such beings, they are truly driving their bodies to a transcendent state, even if they will have to pay for the rest of the week. When I see couples ready to embark on the bliss abyss, I really LOVE them; I love them more than I love almost anything else on the planet. They are going to spend every last cent on having a good time, and they WILL sleep on the hoods of cars, and they WILL dance in public fountains, and they WILL get hypnotized by Keno machines, and they WILL tell their life stories to you if you are open to it, and they WILL feel pain and die painful deaths, but for this moment, they are THE LOVERS, they are what it means to be human in the most rapturous sense, and I salute them.

Idiot Wind Segway

I WAS RIDING MY BIKE up Woodstock and as I finally rounded the top of the hill (huffing and puffing all the way) I saw a man experiencing a moment of cosmic bliss. Yes, it was a dude in full office regalia—a white button-down shirt straining to contain a visible paunch, baggy yet sensible-looking wool-blend pants, gogglebug glasses, and a graying ponytail that clung to the back of his neck like a lovestruck squirrel. He had a bashful, academic air, and he reminded me of Penn of "Penn and Teller" fame.

He was standing upright yet moving forward in space without a single visible muscular twitch. He was cruising along on a Segway—you know, those machines that riot cops and bored househusbands get. They are like the Hummers of the scooter world: steroidal and amoebic at the same time, and looking to me as if they are clumsy, difficult to steer.

So this Ponytail Guy was ZOOMING up the hill, at the very edge of the bike lane, almost veering into the regular car traffic, when along comes a rough red-skinned Motorcycle Papa on a mile-wide Harley.

See him: Crudely tattooed arms, beat-up leather vest, Okefenokee muttonchops and the whole nine yards.

The two men on their respective vehicles were nearly parallel to each other though it was clear that the Harley would overtake Ponytail Guy in seconds.

And what does Ponytail Guy do? He gave a hand signal—yes, a hand signal, of the sort "riders" give other riders—as if to say, "Hey brother, I hear you, I am WITH YOU; our spirits howl like two lone wolves in the wilderness of this Armageddon Planet."

Cancer T-shirt

I'VE GOT A FUNNY ONE. Or is it funny? On a bus yesterday I saw a woman wearing what I immediately recognized as a CANCER T-SHIRT. She was a huge woman, installed in her seat with the sweet, fleshy presence of a fruitcake. The shirt draped around her like a curtain. There was a pattern on the fabric; not one of T cells and blastulas of genetic distortion, not that kind of visually disturbing reference to cancer, no. What was ALL OVER the SHIRT, I mean HUNDREDS of 'em, were cancer-awareness ribbons. You know the ones I mean? Each type of cancer has a different-colored ribbon-symbol to go with it. Just like yellow ribbons once embodied the wartime sentiment "Bring the boys home," the "ribbon image" has been claimed by the anti-cancer industry. These ribbons are legion! As we all know by now, pink ones are for breast cancer, and white ones are for lung cancer (like the opposite of a black smoker's lung, right?) and blue ones are for unruly testicles, and yellow ones are for rogue bones! This woman's shirt was SWARMING with ribbons in a million different colors. I mean, literally, these ribbons were in different sizes and states of emotion and undress. These ribbons were rendered with a sensitive flair to depict motion, as if they were moving across this woman's voluminous bosom, shoulders, and back like a restless flock of birds. This shirt made me look up a "ribbon awareness chart" to decipher the meanings of the colors when I got home. There are ribbons for every disease under the sun—not just cancer. There is a pink and blue combo-ribbon for infant mortality. There is a zebra-print ribbon for something called

"Stiff Person Syndrome." There is an aqua one for Hepatitis C, and a teal one for agoraphobia. There is a red one for AIDS, and green one for Lyme disease. While NOTHING can trump the genetically modified pale pink Breast Cancer Awareness Pumpkins I saw last year, gourds that in their irregular contours accurately mimicked the shape of a cancerous breast, this T-shirt comes...pretty close.

Morgue-Memory

IT WAS FIVE PEE-EM and Rochester, New York was coated in ice, an ice so thick it made you feel your feet were as inarticulate as a baby; your mind was spun in Saran Wrap. I had taken to sneaking into the hospital, haunting the halls, and looking in cabinets and drawers of various doctors. The day came when I discovered the morgue. I didn't know why it was unlocked or unattended. It happened so quickly that it was like a dream; the building, a vast hive of humming machinery; the sort of density that makes ears ring. And hanging in the dark room were bodies in plastic bags. They were hung like dry cleaning, with vises, like huge pairs of pliers, in each dead person's ear-sockets. Who knew a body could so effectively be held up by its skull? Who knows what torments the dead and mute can endure because they have passed beyond torment? I was so fixated on the hanging ones that it took me a moment to realize I was next to a naked fat man who bore more than a passing resemblance to Jim Morrison. He was dead. He was fat. He was young enough. His chest was exposed and a hospital sheet barely covered his loins. I was thinking of walking deeper into the room when I heard footsteps. In a room across the hall I saw a doctor in scrubs, mask, leaning over instruments of his trade. He was about to perform an autopsy. A winter muffler was over my face to hold back the smells. Combat boots were on my feet. I could see that the doctor was going to turn, enter the room of the dead and retrieve one. With every muscle in my body on fire, I sprinted out of that room and down the hall and through a maze of many hallways, until I was out in the dark-ice-night, where air the temperature of meat freezers could revive me, return me to the world of ILLUSION.

Nuclear Winter

"HOW DO YOU LIKE THIS WORD? Nuclear Winter? How do you like this word? Freezing to death? How do you like them together? Nuclear Winter? Freezing to death! On February twenny-fourth, twenny thirty-six, that's the end, that's when the world is going to end. I don't care, I have my wife in the Justice Center."

His apple-red face is full of pores as big as moon craters. While he wears a hood on his head, a mass of dirty blond hair sticks out at odd angles, frozen like stalactites by a personal grease. His body is stocky, long, Nordic in its girth, those massive ski-stick legs in dirty pale denim, pale eyes, pale biceps. Windbreaker B.O., hiking boots turned into sponges in the rain.

His oratory goes on. It is a drunken voice that feels all too familiar to me:

"I met my girlfriend in freshman year math class in nineteen eighty-one. Cleveland High School, I still love her, love her still. She's in the Justice Center. The world's going to end in twenny thirty-six but I don't care as long as I got my wife, my wife. I got a direct line to God. Only a fantasy! This is a fantasy! Ricardo Montalban Island. Dee plane! Dee plane! Welcome to Fantasy Island, Ricardo Montalban is gone, the Wrath of Khan, he put us on this planet twenny-five years ago...Life has changed, never mind! James Teeeee Kirk! Only a movie, let's talk about reality! If I don't get my wife, my wife I came back for her. Everything I do in this life is for her, make her happy."

He says it like a prayer: My wife, my life.

"Share my wife with another man...that makes her happy, then okay!"

I stay on the bus longer just to hear him, peer at his red face, feel where his words are going.

He really does get off at the Justice Center, a real place with a comic-book name, the jail, the courts, the monolith. This is all a fantasy, but it won't end in 2036.

I would do anything for my wife too, if I had one. The buildings are occluded with fog.

Man-Juice
Bicarbonated

TOTALLY HARASSED BY two nineteen-year-old dude-goons with brush cuts in the supermarket. They both looked as dewy as pussywillows with their facial down having just coalesced into the man-billboard of clubber-beard. One was a Latin Lothario pipe cleaner and the other, an Irish inverted triangle of workout man-meat. In Chinese sweatshop cotton sheaths barely stitched to their torsos, they exuded an uncharacteristically persistent enthusiasm. They came on to me SIX TIMES...I mean I brushed these dudes off at least six times and they kept contriving ways to approach me again in each aisle. They wanted to know if I shopped here often and if I lived around here and if they could ask my name and then they ducked around each aisle to find me AGAIN and AGAIN asking which products to buy and in one last-ditch effort asking me if I could help them find the champagne.

One of the late-night stockers, a guy I previously immortalized in here by saying he is the spitting image of a young Edgar Allan Poe, he happened to be near them and I pointed him out and said, "He can show you where the champagne is."

"But he's not as pretty as you," Irish man-meat said.

I figured I could wait them out, and my shopping pace became leisurely. I mean how many times CAN guys be rejected before they move on? DO they realize that even if I don't look it, I am old enough to be their MOTHER????

I didn't lose them by the sugar, the tea, or the macaroni. I didn't lose them in the frozen aisle or by the bargain rack. I thought as I ducked into the self-check area that I finally dodged their chromosomal frenzy, but they came back and told me their names and begged me to say hi to them next time they'd show up.

Where are all the Brittanys and Courtneys these Jadens and Kaydens usually acquire? Another young couple oily with beach tans made out against a magazine rack. Nerds in camo jackets marched through and the late-night stockers, ghostly syphilitic things, maintained a nearly transparent watch on their boxes of Uncle Ben's rice and canned anchovies, having no need to take notice of my plight. I went out of my way to check on the price of some raspberries thinking that my paramours would have to wait too long and give up, but NO, these guys really LINGERED!!

Their ultimate last-ditch effort was to ask me if I had a corkscrew, and I said no.

...Of course they were hoping to enter the brothel I must live in, a mansion of sumptuous boudoirs full of pheasant feathers and lime juice, populated mainly by a Dolly Partonesque menagerie of scattered undergarments that must inevitably coat the floor and every other surface until they resemble the excrudescence of a nest of half-dead beetles. Surely, this would be our collective fate!

But no, they had to finally give me their parting leers and slink away. I gave the magazine rack a leisurely browse to make more distance between myself and these dudes. I'd still have a walk home, and as I made my way out the sliding doors in military strides, I imagined the dudes waiting in a white minivan blasting techno and waiting, waiting under a Christmas-tree cockpit deodorizer for a glimpse of me in their rear-view mirrors.

I passed several bars, and the crematorium thermometer, and a lot of men closer to my age, and I thought I caught, in a side street for a second, the hunky shoulders of these boyos speaking in loud voices, "Why didn'cha just ask her OUT???" and I kept on striding, Amazon powerwalk to my front door peeking at each passing car and wondering if they had given up yet, or would their minivan of man-juice be slowing at a traffic light, man-juice bicarbonated waiting for the only and eternal chance to explode.

The moral of our story?? Anyone who thinks that modern men are evolving into a wispy, sexless troupe of goateed narcissists in satin jackets who fantasize about eating burritos off the bellies of tattooed lesbian housecleaners, the sort of men who, after having sex with a woman, thank her for "opening her petals," can think again! Testosterone is alive and well in the "Youth Set"!

Magic Gardens

MAGIC GARDENS IS PACKED because this historic strip bar is about to close. I call it a jukebox more than a strip bar because to be honest it is where nerds dressed like rednecks come to see bookish women stand on their heads in slow motion to bands like Bauhaus and Thin Lizzy. I mean, I have rarely seen a woman in Magic Gardens strip! It is not that kind of place. The women sway slowly to hip music and lean on things, revealing the edges of their G-stringed labia-lands to a bunch of guys they WOULD consider going home with, and of course there is the rare Russian mobster or elder-goon in need of an oxygen tent.

I used to know the bouncer there, a guy named Abe, and I did a "splosh" photo shoot with him where I ended up covered in whipped cream and frosting in a cold dim living room, a green polka-dot dress stained with corn syrup hiked to my neck.

I had never been in this house before, and never was again. It was on a block of cottages covered in vines. The living room smelled like phantom cat. In my intestines, a serving of half-digested fried mushrooms did their own striptease in a pool of hydrochloric acid. Before the shoot, Abe (mainly for his own edification, I reckon) bought me a lap dance at Union Jack's, and I sat in my best impersonation of Bull Dyke or Indiana Jones, my legs spread as I eyed my lap-dance pet with a benign appraisal.

The girl was a chubby blonde from the rural zones who spent a lot of time rolling her long velvet breasts above my thighs, happy that she had a girl, just a girl who didn't care, and she talked to me about her love of Marilyn Manson, even grabbing a booklet of CDs (post-pussy-exertion) to show me which Marilyns she had.

This is an example of my twenties for you. I jumped at any chance to be half-naked on a stage or in a camera lens, covered in goo. This happened to be a shoot for a pay-per-view site. Abe asked me what I wanted my online "persona" to be called, and I said "Abra Cadabra."

I remember the feeling of cleaning up afterwards and going home, a cloudy winter morning on the 8 bus line with morning work commuters and a bag of frosting-covered clothes tucked under my arm. No one would know what was in my bag...however I was too tired to derive a thrill from my secret.

Mannequinwigbus

I FIRST NOTICE THE MIDDLE-AGED MAN with Truman Capote's face, a baseball cap, and a nondescript utility jacket tenderly holding the styrofoam head on which a foot-high blonde wig is displayed. He is attempting to text at the same time he holds his mannequin head; he is a modern multitasker. The wig is very big, very much like an Afro, but the waves are looser, like the hair of Dolly Parton in the year 1981, back when she still starred in Burt Reynolds movies, back when he had a *face*, and back before she became an anorexic.

This wig, I keep looking at it. I even take two phone pictures of it.

Across from New-Truman is a man on a motorized scooter who is reading a book out loud to the bus. He has greasy mid-period Brando hair and a jawline that reminds me of the pre-cancer Roger Ebert. He has homeless man stench and the book he is reading from is rendered in big type, like a romance novel or a sword and sorcery brick, or maybe new age inspirational; the big-type possibilities are nearly endless.

I have a soggy bag of fish and chips on my seat. It is a rare moment where I am being the PERSON ON THE BUS WITH THE OBNOXIOUS-SMELLING FOOD and it blots out the scent of Homeless Ebert Scooter crotch, though not entirely.

It is then that the scooter man puts down his book and starts talking to New-Truman wig guy. He says, "I used to have poltergeists in me for a long time but now they are long gone and I am reading a book and hold down a job and everything's okay." He proceeds to tell New-Truman about how the wig reminds him of an actress, a

Hollywood actress (which ones aren't?) and she was in a scene of a movie with a green umbrella and it was just beautiful and her hair was like this wig. An image of the young leonine Barbra Streisand fills my head, but I doubt that poltergeist-scooter-dude was thinking of her.

Seated next to New-Truman is Sport Guy. Sport Guy looks all used up, like a piece of baloney that has been left out in the rain, its juices waterlogged and drained away. His body is petite and bony, yet he wears a baseball cap and an athletic shirt and shorts (it's only forty-five degrees) and all of his athletic gear is old, as if it was taken from the seventies even though this man is not more than thirty-eight. His hair is brown and his sneakers look like un-ripened bananas, entire bunches of them on each foot. His eyes are a flat brown color, as if these are discs implanted in a mask of tasteless baloney.

He presses buttons on his phone, a disconcerting mannequin. All of us or none of us are partially alive.

Wyoming

I WAS ON 82ND AVENUE TODAY and for those of you in the know, 82nd Avenue is where a person with eyes can routinely viddy the contents of thousands of heavy metal lunch tables from 1988 roaming like emaciated herons in acid-washed finery, on the lookout for disused hubcaps and stray baby strollers that might fetch ten bucks at a garage sale. This is where the finest Craigslist ads of Portland, OR are formulated... looking for a half-used carton of baby formula, genuine silver tongue jewelry, or fifty-two cars fished out of ditches with sparkling red paint jobs? Looking for a ten-way with perks or a motorcade of Middle Earth Henry Rollins wannabes on a heat-seeking mission for the best crackhouse to hold up and git some bitches? Looking for exotically dressed Russian bag ladies and Nigerian queens? Look no further. Money is tight and the dream of leaving the street let alone the city has evaporated long ago. Roving, wall-eyed lacks of funds are the norm...which is why this is the perfect street to see the Wyoming Board of Tourism place a billboard showcasing the scenic wonders of the rock formations you and your entire family can climb to the top of to enact a little mass suicide ritual if you so desire. Why not? The extremities of nature bring out the extremities of the human soul. I am positive that the folks way back in Wyoming didn't know their billboard would be placed in the middle of a strip of pawn shops, sex shops, and bus stops to eternity. There is probably a Frank Zappa song in here somewhere, but I never really liked Frank Zappa, other than his song "Dirty Love." If I want to hear the sound of an egg beater masturbating, well, I can listen to an egg beater masturbating. You know it happens all the time.

It's All Fun and Games Until

THE OTHER DAY I SAW a teenaged girl at the bus stop repeatedly throw her cell phone on the ground to show her friends how indestructible it was. I'm sure she wouldn't like anyone to do that to her.

Min

SHE WAS A FURTIVE CREATURE in dark blue sweatpants, her hair in a bun, her feet in socks in sandals in a room full of the fumes of dry things: tubes of paint, clay, baloney. My friend Ross kept telling me I had to meet her, see her, peep at her paintings. He said she was a brilliant abstract expressionist, and in the way he had of making every human being sound like a quaint tattered rag doll, he said I just had to look at how dumpy she was and boggle at how such paintings could come out of a sad sack like that.

Ross and I were both in our thirties. He was getting an art degree, and I visited him in the PSU painting studio with its high ceilings and fluorescent lights and the view outside the windows of people smoking on concrete under maple trees. Even with the impending doom of missed deadlines and failing grades, people seemed to move in slow motion, as if they were embroidered on the sidewalks, cups of triple macchiatos in their hands.

Min looked like she was in her later thirties or early forties, her black hair streaked with veins of white, the worry lines that had formed around her mouth and eyes in a bloated moon-shaped face.

I did not see Min drink any triple macchiatos. Min was poor. Min was on a leash. She and her husband moved from China, and they were poor there, let alone here. Her husband was her master, so much so that he didn't know she was taking these art classes. Every day, so Ross told me, Min told her husband that she was going shopping for groceries, or taking a walk. She would sneak around

185

his work schedule, use whatever excuse would work for the day, so that he would not know she was in painting classes.

She had secretly saved the money, over a course of YEARS, to take these painting classes. Her husband knew that she had talent, but he held firm to the ideological position that art for one's emotional edification was wrong and a waste of time. If one was going to condescend to doing something as frivolous as art, it would have to be to make money.

What this meant was that four days a week Min was covered in a cold sweat, in fear of being found out, and in anticipation of losing herself in each of these paintings—phantasmagoric scenes of hell-pits, naked women on fire, and ghostly creatures creeping through forests full of fog; a world of rites, biting, bloodletting, skin-shed-release.

I tried talking to Min about her life, but the language barrier was too much. I have always been terrible at deciphering what people are saying through thick accents. Min knew that her grasp of English was no more than that of a child. The sentences we exchanged were accompanied by smiling and nodding, hands shrugging and eyebrows raised in empathy, as we both expressed the failure of words to be understood by either of us.

Yet Min thirsted for escape. Min gave me and Ross her email address. Min hoped to have friends who understood her love of fairy tales and horror and bliss. None of this came through her words—it bled through the PAINTINGS, which she rolled up every day in cardboard tubes and hid under her mattress so that her husband would never discover they were made.

Summertime came. Ross and I never wrote to Min, and we casually wondered if we would ever run into her again. Ross decided to sell a bunch of his paintings—bold brut portraits of melting souls on hunks of wood—at the Alberta Street Art Fair, a nightmare of gutterpunk clown parades, artisan ice cream eaten by Intel employees, and anarchist noise jams. The street gets clogged by people in fringe and crochet "festival clothing," by dude-bros accompanying their darkwave-for-a-week girlfriends in a stoned shuffle.

We hauled the paintings in and out of Ross' car, arranging them on a sidewalk, and waited for members of the zombie shopper legion to slow in their grazing and ask questions.

But the thing is this: While looking for an empty spot on the sidewalk to set up the paintings—sidewalks that were filled, first-come-first-serve, with hippies selling beads and leather gear and dreamcatchers and graffiti paintings of dogs sipping tea in bondage gear—we sighted something heart-wrenching:

Min. She was with her husband. She was standing up by a row of paintings while her husband sat like a bored overseer in a folding chair. He was tall and older than her, his wavy hair turning Moses-white. He wore a Members Only-style jacket even though the temperature was eighty degrees. Next to Min, a crudely written piece of cardboard said: "Master Paintings —Inquire for Prices"

Propped at Min's weary feet were horrific renditions of Mickey Mouse and Goofy. These were TERRIBLE things that looked like they were created at gunpoint by a handful of ex-cons. I can only describe these renditions of Disney characters and bouquets of flowers as looking like semi-completed Paint by Numbers works—the sort where someone gets the Paint by Numbers set as a Christmas present, and starts executing one, but gets bored before the thing is done.

And how CAN one maintain interest in a Paint by Numbers canvas? Where is the mystery? The picture is already there! The paintings lined up like a row of suspects at Min's feet bore no resemblance to the REAL masterworks that Ross and I had seen her create in the studio. These canvases looked hastily done, almost deliberately without talent, perhaps to convince her husband that she would never be a serious painter. All the better to cover her tracks!

But the thing was, as Min's body stood there by the row of sweat-shop paintings, her sweatpants wrinkled, her sandals lean with wear, where was her mind? Was any part of her embarrassed to be standing by these commercial slop-jobs that in no way represented her inner nature? Or was she simply relieved that she was doing one more thing that would keep her husband from yelling at her, perhaps hitting her?

Years passed. I saw Min in the supermarket line, her husband using the self-checkout machine while she stood, tiny and cloudlike, at his side. As it was at the Alberta Street Art Fair, Min acted like she didn't recognize me. Ross and I both noticed that she had to pretend not to know us under her husband's watch. Talking to visibly weird American Art People would blow her cover!

I used the self-checkout next to Min and her husband, discreetly packed my items in a bag, and scurried into the minefield of the night, where all secrets are contained until they are not.

Wise-Woman

THERE WAS A MAN on the Max who said that his grandmother was a Native American shaman, and she warned him, on the day when he got his archaeology degree, that he must not go on digs where human bones were unearthed. She told him this: Death clings to human bones differently than it clings to the bones of coyotes and other animals.

He was forbidden to approach human bones for what lay in wait. So the man became a drunk and a drifter and went into logging instead. Death clings to logs differently.

Event Horizon

MOST OF THE VINTAGE RETAIL JOBS I've had involved my rear end propped on abnormally high stools over glass cases of non-jewels, listening to men confess their crimes and secret desires to me. One such man, he had a name like Pendergrast, or maybe it was Pinkwater. He was petite and Jewish and tidy in business attire. He was so meticulous in his grooming and even the lines of his eyeglasses, that I could easily imagine that instead of a heart in his chest, he was kept alive by the notched and polished cogs of a Swiss timekeeping device. Pinkwater-Pendergrast would come into the store and tell me how much standing in these aisles, between perfectly starched and ironed (and in some cases, shaved) clothing, brought him back to his childhood. The store had blood-red walls and specialized in fifties and early-sixties attire.

The hallmark of this store was its antiseptic neatness. To me it equated with a sense of suffocation, so I was privately amused when certain customers felt deeply, inwardly consoled by the mad order, as if their souls were so full of holes that a cosmetic display of objects could serve as a stopgap, a life support before the moment of complete implosion.

I was thirty-four years old and had begun an affair with a coke-head who wanted to start a commune. He rarely bathed. Whenever my boyfriend (I hesitate to say "boyfriend," due to how dislocated we were from each other) showed up in the store, he would lean against a particular mirror and cover it with a slurry of sweat. It was such a slurry of sweat that it looked like an aquatic animal had invaded the room and masturbated against the long, cold plate of glass.

I would usually start windexing these smears away while the offender was still in the room. I knew, as I knew in most of my relationships, that what turned me on about men were the parts of their personalities that were unique, and probably forever untouchable to my feelers. The cokehead was also a pot dealer, and though not poor, he conserved his profits for more coke. I had the feeling, despite what he tells me to this day, that he was ultimately more comfortable with drugs than a living woman. He preferred having the option of a woman close by, just in case at a random moment, perhaps once every few weeks, he might emerge from a darkened chamber and require a truly unpredictable reaction, one that he couldn't find on websites dedicated to conspiracy wonkery and soul music 45s.

But back to Pinkwater-Pendergrast; back to the way he seemed to soft-shoe into the store and regale me with tales of his father's upholstery business. Because this store had two customers at the most come in each hour, the man was able to discourse at length on the materials used in each sofa that passed through the San Francisco department store his father worked in as a child. He described the richness of floral tapestries, the tightness of stitches, of rivets, the oils used to keep industrial-strength sewing machines operational. He would ask me why I worked in this vintage store when I was clearly an "intellectual." He asked if I had a boyfriend, and if the boyfriend took me dancing. I would offer a wry smile, and say "yes," and "no."

In my head, I pictured the man I dated. He was all exoskeleton. He was an INSECT in the dingy basement where he lived, a basement so covered in soot from the smoking of marijuana that the carpet had turned a shade of off-black, and the walls could be scraped for resin.

Ballroom dancing, salsa dancing, even meat-market dancing? I had to laugh to myself at Pinkwater-Pendergrast's misconception of my aspirations in this life.

There is one thing I want to get to about this man, Pinkwater-Pendergrast: The reason I bring him up is because of something he said to me during one visit. It has stuck with me for many years.

191

It hasn't just *stuck*—it has haunted me, because in this man's words, I recognized a truth I was actively denying.

When I was in my early twenties, I traveled a lot. I was used to sleeping in parks and on a different stranger's floor each night. I had a lot of personal defects, and the challenges I faced when traveling helped strengthen me in ways I needed to become strong.

During my travels, I came to this conclusion: With looks, identity, and belongings, it is best to remain free. It is DEATH to commit to any idea for so long that one grows inward, so small of mind that one loses the ability to feel how large the world is beyond one's room, one's beliefs, one's house.

While traveling, I felt a drunkenness to drop into a new city and not know where to go. My blood flowed; my mind jarred out of my skull! I felt MORE THAN ALIVE to smell new smells, see new colors of pavement, skin, sex. Every single time I overcame laziness, I was rewarded by adventure on the other side.

So this is what Pinkwater-Pendergrast said:

He felt an urgency to move out of Portland. He was moving back to the Bay Area. Portland was too meager, too small. I couldn't agree more! He said he was thirty-eight years old, and if he stayed here even one more year, he would grow too old, too lazy to pack his belongings and leave. He said that like the land of the lotus-eaters, there were too many comforts in this city, with its clean water, its "just enough" of the arts and liberal thinking.

Of course, whenever he would give me this spiel, he would add that he had investments, big plans, room in his life for a beautiful woman like myself.

But, no! I had my own time bombs to face, and they did not involve Pinkwater-Pendergrast!

I think of the pinched man who perhaps became unstuck to find a new illusion. He was not attractive to me, yet his words lingered like the most potent pheromone.

I think of the phrase "event horizon." I think of the amount of rocket fuel needed to propel a body out of the gravity of a black hole. At a certain point, a falling body can get too close to the edge, the place where matter ceases to make sense—and escape is no longer physically possible.

At some point he stopped coming into the store, and I knew he was gone.

Tiptoe

THERE ARE MOMENTS WHERE I feel the need to tiptoe. We all have. I learned to tiptoe as a child because I liked to stay up all night writing and drawing pictures. I would sneak down to the basement and play records, very softly, trying not to wake up my grandparents. This didn't always work. Once my grandfather got up and started prowling around in the dark with a baseball bat because he thought there was an intruder. I held my breath, crouched under a table for half an hour, until I heard him go back to bed, heard the resonant snoring of his sleep-breath.

I guess I didn't want to surprise him by speaking, or even joking that it was "just me." My child-self figured that the sudden appearance of my voice would be worse than the silence; any interaction might give him a heart attack.

I must have memorized the location of every creak of every floorboard in that house, the variations of sound in the wood from winter to humid summer, and back again.

All of my life I've tiptoed around roommates and lovers, because I veer toward the nocturnal, as if night-juice is my blood, night-sight is what my eyeballs do. Night is the color of my mind.

The thing is this. Now listen, because there is a lesson in here that somehow applies to all of life as we know it:

Often in the course of tiptoeing, one gets into uncomfortable positions, and one gets nervous that one will be heard, so one makes false moves, and stumbles, trips, WHACKS against everything. I don't know how many bruises I've gotten because I tiptoed the wrong way, or tried to rush through narrow openings of doors without swinging them further open in a way that would make hinges creak.

So what is the lesson, you may ask? Well, I have done some of the loudest, stupidest, clumsiest things in my life, in the act of trying to hide the fact that I am moving, that I exist.

Flypaper

AT ONE OF THE LOWEST POINTS of my life, I lived with a man who simmered with violence like a vat of acid, a beaten teen. I never knew when I would do something that would make a conflict occur. Sometimes it could be something as innocent as cleaning out a cat litter box. I would carefully make sure that no urine contacted my hands or clothing, yet when I completed my task, he would claim for hours that he could smell urine on me and that he could not work or think or sleep or act because I had ruined his day with urine. I would calmly say, "I don't want a problem," and wash my hair and change my clothes, because these were the only acts that would keep the rage from boiling over. In many ways I stopped living, stopped leaving, because it was best to not give any provocation, whether the offense was the content of my writing, or the people I might speak to. As winter passed and the summer months grew closer, there were insects in the house. The kitchen was raided by several generations of fast black ants, and the man I was with tried to make humane traps for them, like sugar syrup, jam, honey, candy poured and crushed on the ripped-open envelopes of neglected utility bills. He would get up several times a night to check on the ant traps, so that he could carry the ants outside, leave them by the front door. He did the same in the basement with a population of fruit flies. He dug them out of a cat's water bowl and carefully dried the wings of each fruit fly, an operation that took place on a nearly microscopic scale, requiring great care, and tweezers, and time. After drying each fruit fly, he placed it with its brethren on long strips of toilet paper.

Days would pass and I would see a battlefield of dozens of drowned fruit fly corpses on these strips of toilet paper, strips grown ragged with the moisture and doting. These were the ones that "didn't make it." Each day, the man would convince me that several actually did revive, and that this technique was in fact saving lives. I told the man for two years that I could not live with him, but he refused to leave, and he remained the guardian of the ants and flies and real estate. I wished for a moment that he could treat me with as much respect as he treated these mindless beasts. I was afraid, afraid to my core, and didn't know what to do but hide this fear from myself. You see, he saw me as the enemy, humans as the enemy. He was safe in the realm of flies and ants.

Follow Me Now

12:07 A.M.: THE LAST BUS of the night. The driver is an old greaser—he looks like he's in his mid-sixties, too young to be a fifties leather greaser, and too old to be an eighties punk greaser, but just right for being a sixties-seventies Portland, Oregon greaser, as this is Twin Peaks territory and not much sixties psychedelia ever really happened here. His face is like a handsome Walter Matthau; his face has a touch of the Irish—he's more Irish than Walter Matthau, anyway. With his bulbous nose, his twinkling eyes and his heavy coif of stiff gray hair, he is hanging in there, in the old mortality game, with panache.

I am the only person on the bus. It is a monsoon outside, the kind of night where people don't even trek out to bars. The last bar I was in, a forty-something librarian-looking woman was bemoaning the state of the space program with a middle-aged ponytail man who bore more than a passing resemblance to a walrus. The two were getting increasingly animated, talking about Russia, and rockets blowing up mid-launch, and the waste of billions of dollars on ill-fated attempts at faulty science. I would have stayed to eavesdrop on their space-passion more, but hey, the last bus is the last bus and I don't want to walk three hours home. I could easily imagine this space program conversation morphing into desperate minivan sex and the tepid, uncomfortable yet stoned watching of Nickelodeon cartoon shows for the "irony," but whatever, you know. Motion is good.

I was only on the bus for two stops. The driver yelled that this was his last stop, and I'd have to transfer to another bus that was in front of him. I wasn't sure I heard him right, so I, with my soggy leopard-print coat and my mane of mascara-hair, I walked up to where he was sitting.

"You said I have to transfer to another bus?"

"Yeah, the other nineteen. The bus that was supposed to be here had a breakdown, but she's back on the road. Hey, I'm sorry." He leaned toward me confidentially with his impeccable greaser's quiff. His eyes especially twinkled at this moment. His face bore the markings of a lifetime of heavy drinking. "That driver though, I gotta warn you, she's out of her mind, crazy."

As his bus slowed to a stop, it passed the bus I was about to get on. I saw that the driver was a woman I have ridden with several times in the past. She's the most reckless driver and the most GORGEOUSLY obnoxious borderline schizo I have ever seen hired by Trimet, our city bus service. She is like a mini-gestapo, interrogating passengers on whether their transfers are good, often offering psychological advice, and loudly singing the names of each stop before we reach them. She cannot be quiet. She drives a bus like Han Solo drives his space cruiser. She may be a dyke or she may simply be from Staten Island. Her accent is from the East, or maybe Chicago. She is from somewhere else and acts like it, and no one knows what to do with her pale blue eyes, her linebacker jaw, her precise, nun-like coif of blonde hair. I love her with all my might, and if I didn't think she was going to one day drive me over the edge of the Ross Island Bridge (I mean this woman really swerves her tonnage) I would want her as my personal chauffeur forever. Hell, even if she was gonna take me over the bridge, I'd want her anyway. She makes dying FUN.

So anyway, I knew who Matthau the greaser was referring to right away. Just a few weeks ago, this "crazy" driver told me she wasn't sure if she should stop for me because she thought I was a prostitute with a john. Hey, I love her. I really do. So I look at my driver and give him my confidential smile and lean close and say, "I know. I've ridden with her several times."

Don't look at me like that, reader. Just because I love her doesn't mean I'm going to pretend she's sane!

I get on, and right away show her my transfer and she gives me an affectionate look and says, "Oh yeah, I know you—you're good," and I sit down toward the back. I always sit down toward the back; it's my habit, because the back is raised several feet higher than the front so it is as if I can look out the windows at the city as if I am on a parade float rather than a funeral barge.

Right away, I realize this is a bad idea because I would be able to eavesdrop on her better if I was closer to the front, but I don't bother to get up. Some normal indie teen gets on, and then another, and as we get closer to the city, a young semi-homeless Bill Murray type of lost guy gets on. He sits right by the driver and they start talking. Well you know this is going to be good.

She drives like a maniac over a bridge and the bus roars so loudly that I can barely hear what the two are saying. The man is tall and lonely, maybe a little bit simple, in a dirty red windbreaker with a dirty yellow nylon backpack, short but wild black hair, and a severe profile, as if Bill Murray were punched in the nose and turned into a Dick Tracy character.

He huddles forward in his seat as he says something about how some buses speed by him and don't notice him, and the driver yaps at him about how you have to pray to the bus drivers as if they are gods, and maybe he didn't pray enough, give enough tribute to the bus drivers.

"You know, I want to help you people. As your god, I really say to myself, 'How can I make things better for you?'"

He jokes along with her, and now I really wish I was closer, but I also don't want to be.

She goes on about how nothing in the world is fair and how in the end what every person has to do is decide what is important.

"You gotta not go crazy about the rest!" she sings. As examples, she cites that someone "violating the sanctity" of her body is important, someone "violating the sanctity" of her property is important, but missing a bus, or not getting a job, "not so important"...and this brings the crushed-faced Bill Murray guy to say this:

"You know, there was a point today where I realized I had a meal, and I said, you know, my life is good. I ate."

"Well, God *bless* you."

And the driver, with her sing-song greasy East-Coast voice full of grit and dismissal and sage wisdom...she kept on saying stuff about her bus breaking down three times in one night. She had a flat tire an hour before. During this time, she ferried us through the downtown blocks. I realized that she and the passenger were both like versions of Bill Murray.

Then the janitors got on. I have seen both of these guys get on the late-late bus for the past twenty years. There used to be a third janitor, a man with a jester cap and a wizard's staff, but he moved on to something else about five years ago.

A couple stops up, by campus, a very old person got on the bus. It was an old lady wearing a security guard's uniform, which had a "Securitas" logo on the puffer-jacket lapel. She had baggy black slacks and sensible black clodhoppers on her feet. Her hair was pulled back in a severe bun, some sort of holster was at her waist, and in the face, especially with her glasses, she bore more than a passing resemblance to Roy Orbison.

This old lady, she was probably sixty years old at the least, and she had bad legs or hips, and whatever was going bad, it caused her to have to walk slowly down the aisle as she made her way, with great dignity, great gravitas, toward the very back seats, where the janitors were.

She smiled—in fact she *melted* as she sat down across from the janitor I always thought of as a real nebbish. This guy she sat with has Coke-bottle glasses and a squeamish look at all times. He is about fifty-five years old, and he is quick to anger and quick to fidget, but when speaking with this grande security dame, he was at ease.

I overheard them. He started telling her about his cat. His cat is nineteen years old but has the energy of a kitten. His cat runs around all the time and waits for him to come home at the bus stop, and when he keeps the cat in at night, the cat wakes him up to let it out so that it can relieve itself of waste in the great outdoors. He made the mistake of letting the cat out *once*, and now the cat expects him to be at its beck and call to let her urinate or defecate at the same time every day, which I think is in his morning, and would probably be three in the afternoon to the rest of you.

He said, "Sometimes I want to say, I love you but you're so annoying I want to throw you out the freakin' window."

All of a sudden, I saw that this guy who seemed for years to be so fidgety and angry about everything had a soft spot for his cat, his nineteen-year-old cat, and I loved him for it. And I loved the old security-guard woman for having the strength to do whatever the hell she did in her security guard uniform. I can only hope no one ever challenges her to stop a thief or a killer for real.

When the bus finally got to my stop, the jovial manic Lord-knows-what driver cheered to me: "You made it! You made it all in one piece!"

I ate today. This is my meal.

Asshole-Ade

WHEN LIFE GIVES YOU ASSHOLES, make asshole-ade.

Appearances Can Be Deceiving, Until They Aren't, 2 a.m.

Outside the QFC grocery store I overheard a tweaker fighting with another man, who in the dimness appeared to be a metalhead or bike messenger. (Isn't that an old-fashioned term? In our technological milieu, do bike messengers even exist anymore?) The PRIME MOVER, PRIME TWEAKER, he was Moses and David Lee Roth put together, which I realize is kind of redundant, saying that a tweaker looks like David Lee Roth. He had a big-jawed face baked terracotta from the sun and a shock of feathered white hair. I suspect it just *grew* this way, but he had a definite pride in this head of hair; how it fluttered and flowed in the stale night air as if he had just posed for the cover of *Teen Beat* magazine.

The sliding doors opened, just as I overheard the metal-ish dude say, "Hey, that's my bike you are taking, that's my bike!"

"You trying to fuck with ME?" Prime Tweaker barked, "You trying to FUCK WITH ME? This is MY bike!" He gripped the handlebars of a hybrid-wheeled cushy titanium-framed bike, which is the equivalent of an old person driving an Audi; comfort all the *way*, baby. "You gonna tell me MY bike is YOUR bike? HUH? HUH?"

Prime Tweaker, his fingers and wrists clogged with plastic bags of collected cans and bottles, he managed to grip the handlebars of the BIG CUSHY BIKE and rattle them in the face of the metal dude, as if he was revving his engines. He was trying to get the guy to back up. He was revving and barking!

The doors slid closed, and I kept watching. I got closer to the doors so that my weight would cue a hidden sensor and trigger them to open again. I wanted to hear more. I didn't care if these guys saw me watching them. A pedestrian in plaid pajama shorts with an office haircut was also stalled on the sidewalk soaking in the dew-dropper wolverine prowl.

Prime Tweaker kept threatening the guy. He dropped his bags and raised his fists, jerking his body back and forth as if he was going to do space-alien jiu-jitsu on the metal man, whose bike was in the process of being "stolen."

As soon as things escalated to a fight, I decided to enter the store and tell one of the late-night stockers what was happening outside the door.

The late-night stocker was one of those ginger-haired boys you think always plays video games and resembles a human Pop-Tart clone just produced from a test tube in a secret bunker in Illinois. He was upended—literally on his back on the floor, removing the innards of one of the always-breaking-apart "self-check" machines.

I knew already that he wouldn't want to know what was happening and wouldn't do anything anyway, but I decided to tell him.

"And they are getting into a fight?" he said, wearily.

"Yep."

"Right in front of the door?"

"Yep."

He sighed. I knew he wouldn't do anything so I reassured him. "It will probably blow over," I said.

I wanted to back out of the situation. Hobbit-Pop-Tart-Man was not going to do anything, and what could he do, anyway? Taser a tweaker? Whack his hand with a metal ruler? Call the cops on him? To do WHAT? Exactly.

I started getting my groceries. Within a minute, the sliding doors opened and I caught the fast-moving form of Prime Tweaker going up and down the aisles.

After a minute, I saw the guy whose bike was apparently being stolen.

Under the fluorescent lights, a sort of powdery fishy malaise that would make even an infant look like a chain-smoking sixty-year-old male nurse, I saw that the "metal dude" was actually far stranger than the outside light could reveal:

He was very tall, well over six feet, with ragged black pants rolled up over ankles that were covered in welts and scabs. His hair, the color of sun-bleached rope, was more matted than I had first noticed. His black cap was threadbare and faded to gray. He had hollows under his eyes like a man who hadn't slept in lifetimes. He didn't look unhealthy; he looked diseased.

Oh God, they BOTH were tweakers! And the one who acted tweakier actually looked healthier than *this* man! Upon seeing him, I could no longer determine whose bike was whose! How many owners of the street, how many sidewalk scarecrow-mitts had this bike passed through, anyway?

I was in a daze, ready to go to sleep and realizing that the main items I came for weren't even in stock (packing tape and hair dye) and Prime Tweaker passed me, at which point he gave me a Groucho Marx eyebrow-raise and made a sort of "Hubba-Hubba" noise that sounded more like, "Hel-lo, Dol-ly!"

At this moment he was godlike; *very* David Lee Roth.

My eyes gulped in the contours of Prime Tweaker's sculpted biceps in a muscle shirt, the extreme whiteness of his eyeballs and his teeth. Yes, he definitely took pride in his looks, and had an aim to snare the ladies...still!

He jerked his way to the checker to trade in his bottles for cash. I sensed that this was the perfect time for me to make my great escape, and avoid any outdoor trysts with Prime Tweaker or the Metal Ichabod Crane.

She Spilled the Blueberries

THERE IS A REASON humans love lists. Lists are visceral; lists satisfy a need for pure information without involving a reader in too many intricacies of plot or musicality. Lists are non sequitur; lists have the element of shock. Lists are like eyesight and the breaking of lightbulbs and kneecaps in alleyways.

Lists like this: The woman with Bob Geldof's face who has one side she makes her boyfriend sit on when they recline on a bench. Why does she choose that side? Is she steering him away from a pimple, or away from the view of an attractive woman's rear end?

Lists of the two homeless men, one mentally damaged and overweight like a rotting ham, and he smells of a thousand years of B.O., and he is carrying all of the bags, as a lean Hunter S. Thompson snake who reeks of smoke and has shorn silver hair barks instructions: "We can take the 19, the 17 or the 9. We then transfer to the Max and walk to the dentistry center."

What??? What are these two guys going to get at the dentistry center at eleven pee-em? What *is* the dentistry center? The big guy led by the barker, he is like a son and a slave and a lover rolled into one. Like Lennie in *Of Mice and Men,* I cannot look at him without imagining small animals being smothered in his palms.

There is the guy who corners me by the overflowing sewer, and he tells me he remembers me from the past and I give him more minutes than I can even believe, as if I owe any human a string of words before I release my final breath. And there is another man who looks like he has had plastic surgery over and over again. He appears to have hair transplants, and Botox, and fillers, and creams, and he is either a twelve-year-old stretched out on rollers, or a sixty-year-old soaked, like a Chinese pickle, in a vat of MSG.

There is the teen romance! Two kids in rave-wear: the girl looks like her barfly mum. How do I know she has a barfly mum? Because she is barely fifteen, and already talks like a fifty-five-year-old ex-stripper, and she moves her head with exhaustion and trouble and childbirth and GIMME SHELTER beyond her years, just like her mum and her grandmum and all of her aunts and the whole gene pool back to Ireland where her face would be that of a faerie queene. Her roots are blonde but the tips are dark auburn and tied in a scraggly braid in which she has planted two plastic flowers. On her legs are psychedelic plastic bell-bottoms that look like they were just purchased from a Halloween store, and her boyfriend, a boy who bears more than a passing resemblance to a pubescent Jackson Browne, he wears shorts with green knee socks that proudly say "WEED ... WEED ... WEED ..." in all caps, like a campaign slogan.

He leans his head close to her shoulder with a silent sigh of love, and I can see he is really the girl and she is really the boy in this scenario, as she talks and he swoons, and hanging from his belt-loop like a sword in its scabbard is a big plastic PARTY BEER MUG that matches his knee socks. Both of these teenaged lovebirds look like they have been awake for two weeks; their eyes are bloodshot and they both wear strange orange vinyl smocks over their torsos that read "Humpin' City." A tiny logo of a naked woman lies beneath the words.

Dose crazy kids!!!

I stop at the grocery store before going home, and in the self-check line a drunk blonde woman with a troll body and a face slowly turning to a chiseled presidential visage on Mount Rushmore nervously eyes the sliding doors to see if her "man"—some guy with a shaved head and cargo shorts—is approaching. She is so drunk that she is moving in slow motion. She is wearing bejeweled thongs on her feet, which showcase the bruised blue-black color of her toenail polish, exactly the color my fingernail turned after I got it stuck in a door last month!

Speaking of blue, this lady spills her carton of blueberries all over the floor and she is for ten seconds mortified, and then wearied, and then both of us laugh as hundreds of blueberries—like crazed kittens or children let out of school—race across the freshly waxed floor. No matter that some migrant worker probably got paid minus-thirty cents an hour to pick these berries, they now race to obscurity at ankle level, and we laugh.

What else can we do? Will either of us pluck these perishables from the killing fields of the supermarket floor and insist they be saved? Several minutes pass and the woman growls, "Does anyone even WORK here?"

In what I assume is embarrassment mixed with impatience, the woman walks away from the scattered population of blueberries which, in their bold, exploratory patterns, make us humans look timid in comparison.

Holes

IN THE PARTY FAVOR STORE a tweaker lady, nude under a pair of overalls, rakes her hands through a rustic basket of individually wrapped hard candies. She is all of twenty-three, with the memories of a crone. These candies can plug the holes where her soul leaks out, one man at a time, one car, one sofa cushion. Clouds and blue sky shine out of her holes. I see vistas where there was once a child.

Death Roofie

I HAVE HYPNOTIZED MYSELF long ago. I shook hands with death, French-kissed death. We have our separations, our little grudges, but we always get back together in the end. Death just texted me! How'd death know I was writing this? Instinct! Death insists that I have consummated the relationship many times now, but I just don't remember. Death must have given me a roofie.

Nine-Eleven

I WAS ASLEEP WHEN I got a phone call from a noise musician who said: "Hey, ya gotta turn on your tee-vee. It's really cool...like, things are blowing up!"

I turned on my tee-vee. It was surreal. Most of the people I was close to at the time desperately hoped civilization would end, and their minds—like yolks from eggs, like a network of busted capillaries, like violent pink blooms from the tight green fists of buds—would be blown.

I watched people jumping out of mile-high windows, bodies so small that they looked like pieces of paper in the sky, white confetti, death confetti.

My life is different now.